Worthington George Smith, George Bentham

Illustrations of the British flora

A series of wood engravings, with dissections, of British plants. Second Edition

Worthington George Smith, George Bentham

Illustrations of the British flora

A series of wood engravings, with dissections, of British plants. Second Edition

ISBN/EAN: 9783337107574

Printed in Europe, USA, Canada, Australia, Japan

Cover: Foto ©Andreas Hilbeck / pixelio.de

More available books at **www.hansebooks.com**

ILLUSTRATIONS

OF

THE BRITISH FLORA:

A SERIES OF

WOOD ENGRAVINGS, WITH DISSECTIONS,

OF

British Plants,

DRAWN BY

W. H. FITCH, F.L.S.,

AND

W. G. SMITH, F.L.S.

FORMING AN ILLUSTRATED COMPANION TO MR. BENTHAM'S HANDBOOK AND OTHER BRITISH FLORAS.

SECOND EDITION, REVISED AND ENLARGED.

LONDON:
L. REEVE & CO., 5, HENRIETTA STREET, COVENT GARDEN.
1887.

PREFACE

TO THE FIRST EDITION.

THE Illustrated Edition of Mr. Bentham's "Handbook of the British Flora" being exhausted, the Wood engravings of that work are here reproduced as an Illustrated Companion to the " Handbook " and other British Floras. The Cuts are arranged according to the last Edition of the " Handbook," and new Cuts of the species admitted in recent Editions are added. To facilitate reference from other Floras, where the nomenclature differs from that of the " Handbook," synonyms, in italics, are incorporated in the Index. In this volume and the " Handbook " combined, Students will have, in a more convenient and portable form, all that the Illustrated Edition contained, at little more than one-third the cost.

PREFACE
TO THE SECOND EDITION.

The exhaustion of a large Edition of this work in the course of a few years is a gratifying proof of its utility to, and appreciation by, Students of Botany, and has encouraged the Publishers, in preparing a new Edition for the press, to endeavour to render it still more useful and worthy of the patronage it has already received. In the present Edition, five new cuts have been added, and the whole have been rearranged according to the New Edition (the Fifth, just published) of Bentham's " Handbook " as revised by Sir J. D. Hooker. The Index has been greatly enlarged to facilitate reference from other Floras, and a new Index of English and popular names has been added. Lastly, to meet the convenience of Students of limited means, the price of this volume, and also of the Handbook, has been reduced from 12*s*. to 10*s*. 6*d*., the Publishers relying upon an increased sale to compensate them for the surrender thus made. In this volume and the " Handbook " combined, therefore, Students will now have a complete Illustrated British Flora, the best, especially for beginners, for one guinea.

London, *March 22nd*, 1887.

NATURAL ORDERS

ILLUSTRATED IN THIS VOLUME.

	FIGURES		FIGURES
i. RANUNCULACEÆ	1-32	xxxi. REBESIACEÆ	370-373
ii. BERBERIDEÆ	33	xxxii. SAXIFRAGACEÆ	374-389
iii. NYMPHÆACEÆ	34, 35	xxxiii. DROSERACEÆ	390-392
iv. PAPAVERACEÆ	36-44	xxxiv. HALORAGEÆ	393-395
v. FUMARIACEÆ	45-47	xxxv. UMBELLIFERÆ	396-454
vi. CRUCIFERÆ	48-112	xxxvi. ARALIACEÆ	455
vii. RESEDACEÆ	113-115	xxxvii. LORANTHACEÆ	456
viii. CISTACEÆ	116-119	xxxviii. CORNACEÆ	457, 458
ix. VIOLACEÆ	120-125	xxxix. CAPRIFOLIACEÆ	459-467
x. POLYGALACEÆ	126	xl. STELLATÆ	468-481
xi. FRANKENIACEÆ	127	xli. VALERIANEÆ	482-489
xii. CARYOPHYLLACEÆ	128-172	xlii. DIPSACEÆ	490-494
xiii. PORTULACEÆ	173, 174	xliii. COMPOSITÆ	495-609
xiv. TAMARISCINEÆ	175	xliv. CAMPANULACEÆ	610-623
xv. ELATINACEÆ	176, 177	xlv. ERICACEÆ	624-646
xvi. HYPERICINEÆ	178-188	xlvi. PRIMULACEÆ	647-661
xvii. LINACEÆ	189-193	xlvii. LENTIBULACEÆ	662-667
xviii. MALVACEÆ	194-199	xlviii. OLEACEÆ	668, 669
xix. TILIACEÆ	200	xlix. APOCYNACEÆ	670, 671
xx. GERANIACEÆ	201-219	l. GENTIANACEÆ	672-682
xxi. ACERACEÆ	220, 221	li. POLEMONIACEÆ	683
xxii. AQUIFOLIACEÆ	222	lii. CONVOLVULACEÆ	684-689
xxiii. CELUSTRACEÆ	223	liii. BORAGINEÆ	690-710
xxiv. RHAMNACEÆ	224, 225	liv. SOLANACEÆ	711-715
xxv. PAPILIONACEÆ	226-296	lv. OROBANCHACEÆ	716-723
xxvi. ROSACEÆ	297-340	lvi. SCROPHULARINEÆ	724-774
xxvii. ONAGRACEÆ	341-353	lvii. LABIATÆ	775-819
xxviii. LYTHRARIEÆ	354-356	lviii. VERBENACEÆ	820
xxix. CUCURBITACEÆ	357	lix. PLUMBAGINEÆ	821-825
xxx. CRASSULACEÆ	358-369	lx. PLANTAGINEÆ	826-831

	FIGURES		FIGURES
lxi. ILLECEBRACEÆ	832-836	lxxix. ALISMACEÆ	967-975
lxii. CHENOPODIACEÆ	837-855	lxxx. HYDROCHARIDEÆ	976-978
lxiii. POLYGONACEÆ	856-877	lxxxi. ORCHIDACEÆ	979-1014
lxiv. THYMELEACEÆ	878, 879	lxxxii. IRIDEÆ	1015-1021
lxv. ELÆAGNACEÆ	880	lxxxiii. AMARYLLIDEÆ	1022-1025
lxvi. SANTALACEÆ	881	lxxxiv. DIOSCORIDEÆ	1026
lxvii. ARISTOLOCHIACEÆ	882	lxxxv. LILIACEÆ	1027-1057
lxviii. EUPHORBIACEÆ	883-897	lxxxvi. JUNCACEÆ	1058-1079
lxix. EMPETRACEÆ	898	lxxxvii. RESTIACEÆ	1080
lxx. CALLITRICHINEÆ	899-900	lxxxviii. CYPERACEÆ	1081-1154
lxxi. URTICACEÆ	901-905	lxxxix. GRAMINEÆ	1155-1254
lxxii. ULMACEÆ	906, 907	xc. LYCOPODIACEÆ	1255-1259
lxxiii. AMENTACEÆ	908-933	xci. SELAGINELLACEÆ	1260, 1261
lxxiv. CONIFERÆ	934-936		
lxxv. TYPHACEÆ	937-941	xcii. MARSILEACEÆ	1262
lxxvi. AROIDEÆ	942, 943	xciii. EQUISETACEÆ	1263-1272
lxxvii. LEMNACEÆ	944-948	xciv. FILICES	1273-1310
lxxviii. NAIADEÆ	949-966		

ILLUSTRATIONS

OF THE

BRITISH FLORA.

RANUNCULACEÆ.

1. Clematis Vitalba.

2. Thalictrum alpinum

3. Thalictrum minus.

4. Thalictrum flavum.

B

5. Anemone Pulsatilla.

6. Anemone nemorosa.

7. Adonis autumnalis.

8. Myosurus minimus.

9. Ranunculus aquatilis.

10. Ranunculus hederaceus.

RANUNCULACEÆ.

11. Ranunculus Lingua.

12. Ranunculus Flammula.

13. Ranunculus ophioglossifolius.

15. Ranunculus sceleratus.

14. Ranunculus Ficaria.

16. Ranunculus auricomus.

RANUNCULACEÆ.

17. Ranunculus acris.

18. Ranunculus repens.

20. Ranunculus bulbosus.

19. Ranunculus chærophyllos.

21. Ranunculus hirsutus.

22. Ranunculus parviflorus.

RANUNCULACEÆ.

23. Ranunculus arvensis.

24. Caltha palustris.

25. Trollius europæus.

26. Helleborus viridis.

27. Helleborus fœtidus.

RANUNCULACEÆ.

28. Aquilegia vulgaris.

29. Delphinium Ajacis.

30. Aconitum Napellus.

31. Actæa spicata.

NYMPHÆACEÆ.

32. Pæonia officinalis.

33. Berberis vulgaris.

34. Nymphæa alba.

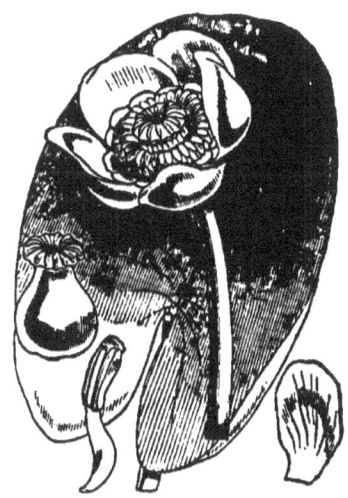

35. Nuphar luteum.

8   PAPAVERACEÆ.

36. Papaver somniferum.

37. Papaver Rhœas.

38. Papaver dubium.

39. Papaver hybridum.

PAPAVERACEÆ.

40. Papaver Argemone.

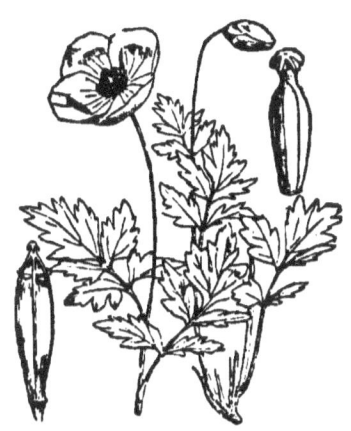

41. Meconopsis cambrica.

42. Chelidonium majus.

43. Rœmeria hybrida.

FUMARIACEÆ.

44. Glaucium luteum.

46. Corydalis lutea.

47. Corydalis claviculata.

45. Fumaria officinalis.

48. Matthiola incana.

CRUCIFERÆ.

49. Matthiola sinuata.

51. Barbarea vulgaris.

50. Cheiranthus Cheiri.

52. Nasturtium officinale.

CRUCIFERÆ

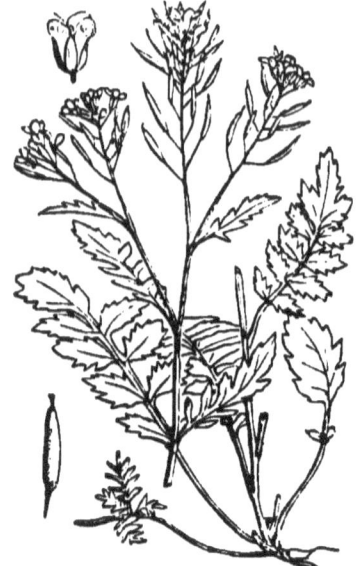
53. Nasturtium sylvestre.

54. Nasturtium palustre.

55. Nasturtium amphibium.

56. Arabis perfoliata.

CRUCIFERÆ.

57. Arabis Turrita.

59. Arabis ciliata.

60. Arabis Thaliana.

58. Arabis hirsuta.

61. Arabis stricta.

CRUCIFERÆ.

62. Arabis petræa.

63. Cardamine amara.

64. Cardamine pratensis.

65. Cardamine impatiens.

CRUCIFERÆ.

66. Cardamine hirsuta.

67. Cardamine bulbifera.

68. Hesperis matronalis.

69. Sisymbrium officinale.

CRUCIFERÆ.

70. Sisymbrium Irio.

71. Sisymbrium Sophia.

72. Alliaria officinalis.

73. Erysimum cheiranthoides.

74. Erysimum orientale.

75. Brassica tenuifolia.

76. Brassica muralis.

77. Brassica monensis.

CRUCIFERÆ.

78. Brassica oleracea.

79. Brassica campestris.

80. Brassica alba.

81. Brassica Sinapis.

CRUCIFERÆ. 19

82. Brassica nigra.

83. Brassica adpressa.

84. Cochlearia Armoracia.

85. Cochlearia officinalis.

c 2

CRUCIFERÆ.

86. Alyssum calycinum.

87. Alyssum maritimum.

88. Draba aizoides.

89. Draba hirta.

90. Draba incana.

CRUCIFERÆ.

91. Draba muralis.

93. Camelina sativa.

92. Draba verna.

94. Subularia aquatica.

95. Thlaspi arvense.

96. Thlaspi perfoliatum.

CRUCIFERÆ.

97. Thlaspi alpestre.

98. Teesdalia nudicaulis.

99. Iberis amara.

101. Capsella Bursa-pastoris.

100. Hutchinsia petræa.

CRUCIFERÆ.

102. Lepidium campestre.

104. Lepidium Draba.

103. Lepidium Smithii.

105. Lepidium latifolium.

CRUCIFERÆ.

106. Lepidium ruderale.

108. Senebiera didyma.

107. Senebiera Coronopus.

109. Isatis tinctoria.

RESEDACEÆ.

110. Cakile maritima.

112. Raphanus Raphanistrum.

111. Crambe maritima.

113. Reseda luteola.

CISTACEÆ.

114. Reseda lutea.

115. Reseda alba.

116. Helianthemum guttatum.

117. Helianthemum canum.

VIOLACEÆ.

118. Helianthemum vulgare.

121. Viola odorata.

119. Helianthemum polifolium.

122. Viola hirta.

120. Viola palustris.

123. Viola arenaria.

POLYGALACEÆ.

124. Viola canina.

126. Polygala vulgaris

125. Viola tricolor.

127. Frankenia lævis.

128. Dianthus prolifer.

CARYOPHYLLACEÆ.

129. Dianthus Armeria.

130. Dianthus deltoides.

131. Dianthus cæsius.

132. Saponaria officinalis.

133. Silene acaulis.

CARYOPHYLLACEÆ.

134. Silene Cucubalus.

135. Silene Otites

36. Silene nutans.

137. Silene gallica.

CARYOPHYLLACEÆ.

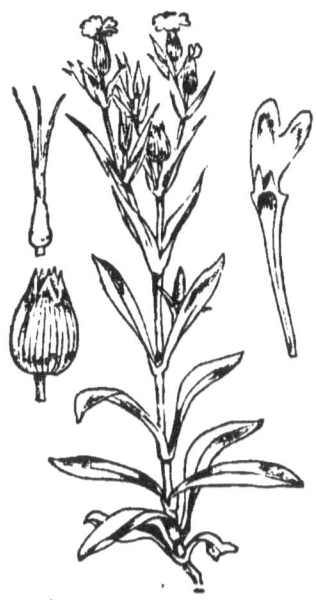

138. Silene conica.

139. Silene noctiflora.

140. Lychnis vespertina.

141. Lychnis diurna.

32 CARYOPHYLLACEÆ.

142. Lychnis Githago.

143. Lychnis Flos-cuculi.

144. Lychnis Viscaria.

145. Lychnis alpina.

CARYOPHYLLACEÆ.

146. Sagina procumbens.

147. Sagina Linnæi.

148. Sagina nodosa.

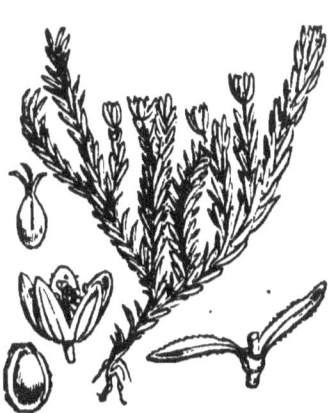

149. · Cherleria sedoides.

150. Arenaria verna.

151. Arenaria uliginosa.

152. Arenaria tenuifolia.

153. Arenaria peploides

CARYOPHYLLACEÆ.

154. Arenaria serpyllifolia.

156. Arenaria trinervis

155. Arenaria ciliata.

157. Mœnchia erecta.

CARYOPHYLLACEÆ.

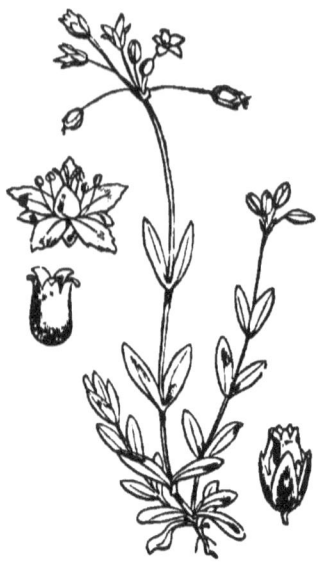

158. Holosteum umbellatum.

159. Cerastium vulgatum.

160. Cerastium arvense.

161. Cerastium alpinum.

162. Cerastium trigynum.

CARYOPHYLLACEÆ.

163. Stellaria aquatica.

165. Stellaria media.

164. Stellaria nemorum.

166. Stellaria uliginosa.

CARYOPHYLLACEÆ.

167. Stellaria graminea.

168. Stellaria palustris.

169. Stellaria Holostea.

170. Spergularia rubra.

PORTULACEÆ.

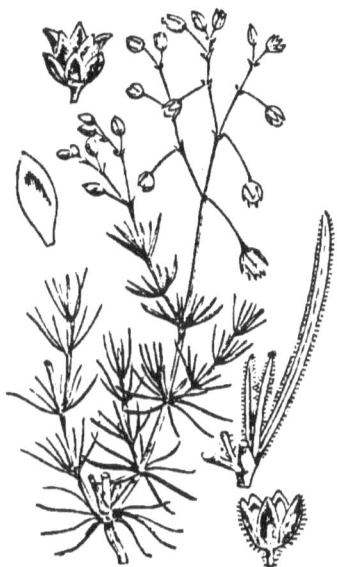

171. Spergula arvensis.

172. Polycarpon tetraphyllum.

173. Claytonia perfoliata.

175. Tamarix gallica.

174. Montia fontana.

ELATINACEÆ.

176. Elatine hexandra.

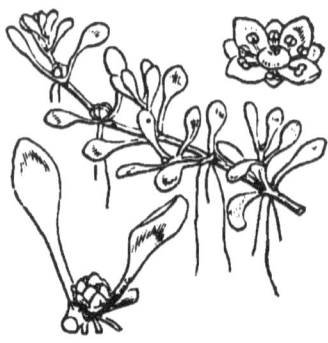

177. Elatine Hydropiper.

178. Hypericum calycinum.

179. Hypericum Androsæmum.

HYPERICINEÆ.

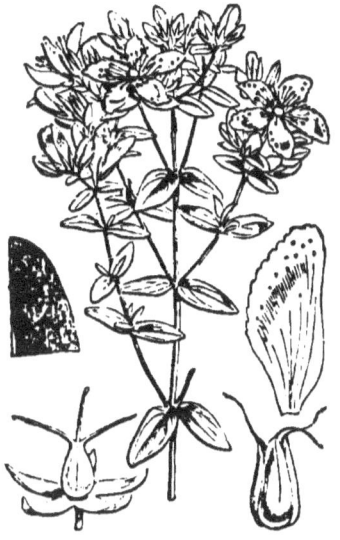

180. Hypericum perforatum.

181. Hypericum dubium.

182. Hypericum quadrangulum.

183. Hypericum humifusum.

184. Hypericum linarifolium.

186. Hypericum hirsutum.

185. Hypericum pulchrum.

187. Hypericum montanum.

LINACEÆ.

188. Hypericum Elodes.

189. Linum usitatissimum.

190. Linum perenne.

191. Linum angustifolium.

LINACEÆ.

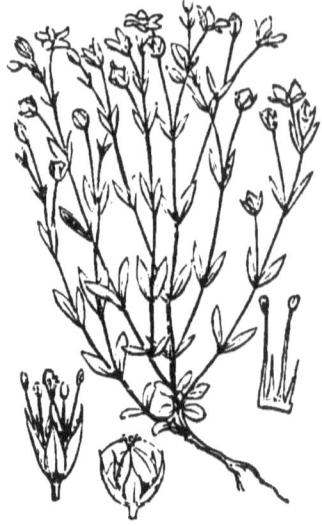

192. Linum catharticum.

193. Radiola Millegrana.

194. Lavatera arborea.

195. Malva rotundifolia.

MALVACEÆ.

196. Malva sylvestris.

198. Althæa officinalis.

197. Malva moschata.

199. Althæa hirsuta.

46   TILIACEÆ.

200. Tilia europæa.

201. Geranium sanguineum.

202. Geranium phæum.

203. Geranium sylvaticum.

GERANIACEÆ.

204. Geranium pratense.

205. Geranium pyrenaicum.

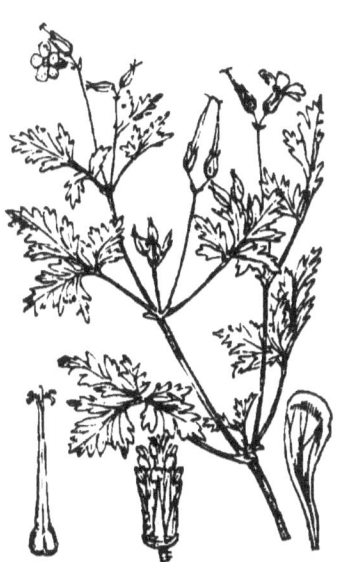

206. Geranium Robertianum.

207. Geranium lucidum.

GERANIACEÆ.

208. Geranium molle

209. Geranium pusillum.

210. Geranium rotundifolium.

211. Geranium dissectum.

GERANIACEÆ.

212. Geranium columbinum.

214. Erodium moschatum.

213. Erodium cicutarium.

215. Erodium maritimum.

E

GERANIACEÆ.

216. Oxalis Acetosella.

218. Impatiens Noli-me-tangere.

217. Oxalis corniculata.

219. Impatiens fulva.

ACERACEÆ.

220. Acer campestre.

221. Acer Pseudo-platanus.

222. Ilex Aquifolium.

223. Evonymus europæus.

RHAMNACEÆ.

224. Rhamnus catharticus.

225. Rhamnus Frangula.

226. Ulex europæus.

227. Ulex nanus.

PAPILIONACEÆ. 53

228. Genista tinctoria.

229. Genista pilosa.

230. Genista anglica.

231. Cytisus scoparius.

PAPILIONACEÆ.

232. Ononis arvensis.

233. Ononis reclinata.

234. Medicago falcata.

235. Medicago sativa.

PAPILIONACEÆ.

236. Medicago lupulina.

237. Medicago denticulata.

238. Medicago maculata.

239. Medicago minima.

PAPILIONACEÆ.

240. Melilotus officinalis.

242. Melilotus alba.

241. Melilotus arvensis.

243. Trigonella ornithopodioides.

PAPILIONACEÆ.

244. Trifolium incarnatum.

246. Trifolium arvense.

245. Trifolium Bocconi.

247. Trifolium stellatum.

PAPILIONACEÆ.

248. Trifolium ochroleucum.

249. Trifolium pratense.

250. Trifolium medium.

251. Trifolium maritimum.

PAPILIONACEÆ. 59

252. Trifolium striatum.

253. Trifolium scabrum.

254. Trifolium strictum.

255. Trifolium glomeratum.

PAPILIONACEÆ.

256. Trifolium suffocatum.

258. Trifolium subterraneum.

257. Trifolium resupinatum.

259. Trifolium fragiferum.

PAPILIONACEÆ.

260. Trifolium repens.

261. Trifolium hybridum.

262. Trifolium procumbens.

263. Trifolium minus.

PAPILIONACEÆ.

264. Trifolium filiforme.

266. Lotus angustissimus.

265. Lotus corniculatus.

267. Anthyllis Vulneraria.

PAPILIONACEÆ. 63

268. Astragalus hypoglottis.

269. Astragalus alpinus.

270. Astragalus glycyphyllos.

271. Oxytropis campestris.

PAPILIONACEÆ.

272. Oxytropis uralensis.

273. Ornithopus ebracteatus.

274. Ornithopus perpusillus.

275. Hippocrepis comosa.

PAPILIONACEÆ.

276. Onobrychis sativa.

277. Vicia hirsuta.

278. Vicia tetrasperma.

279. Vicia Cracca.

F

280. Vicia sylvatica.

281. Vicia Orobus.

282. Vicia sepium.

283. Vicia lutea.

PAPILIONACEÆ.

284. Vicia sativa.

285. Vicia lathyroides.

286. Vicia bithynica.

287. Lathyrus Nissolia.

F 2

PAPILIONACEÆ.

288. Lathyrus Aphaca.

289. Lathyrus hirsutus.

290. Lathyrus pratensis.

291. Lathyrus tuberosus.

PAPILIONACEÆ. 69

292. Lathyrus sylvestris.

293. Lathyrus palustris.

294. Lathyrus maritimus.

295. Lathyrus macrorrhizus.

70 ROSACEÆ.

295. Lathyrus niger.

297. Prunus communis.

298. Prunus Cerasus.

299. Prunus Padus.

ROSACEÆ.

300. Spiræa salicifolia.

301. Spiræa Ulmaria.

302. Spiræa Filipendula.

303. Dryas octopetala.

ROSACEÆ.

304. Geum urbanum.

305. Geum rivale.

306. Rubus Idæus.

307. Rubus fruticosus.

ROSACEÆ.

308. Rubus cæsius.

309. Rubus saxatilis.

310. Rubus Chamæmorus.

311. Fragaria vesca.

ROSACEÆ.

312. Potentilla Fragariastrum.

313. Potentilla reptans.

314. Potentilla Tormentilla.

315. Potentilla argentea.

ROSACEÆ.

316. Potentilla verna.

317. Potentilla fruticosa.

318. Potentilla anserina.

319. Potentilla rupestris.

ROSACEÆ.

320. Potentilla Comarum.

321. Sibbaldia procumbens.

322. Alchemilla vulgaris.

323. Alchemilla alpina.

ROSACEÆ.

324. Alchemilla arvensis.

325. Sanguisorba officinalis.

326. Poterium Sanguisorba.

327. Agrimonia Eupatoria

ROSACEÆ.

328. Rosa pimpinellifolia.

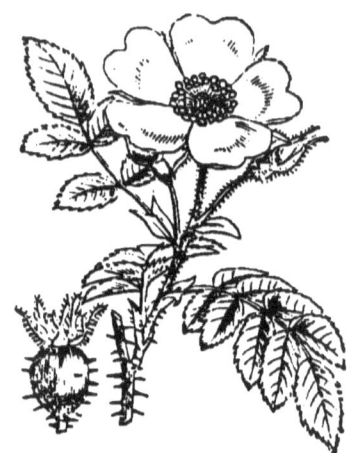

329. Rosa villosa.

330. Rosa rubiginosa.

331. Rosa canina.

ROSACEÆ. 79

332. Rosa arvensis.

333. Pyrus communis.

334. Pyrus Malus.

335. Pyrus Aria.

ROSACEÆ.

336. Pyrus torminalis.

337. Pyrus Aucuparia.

338. Cratægus Oxyacantha.

339. Cotoneaster vulgaris.

ONAGRACEÆ.

340. Mespilus germanica.

341. Epilobium angustifolium

342. Epilobium hirsutum.

343. Epilobium parviflorum.

G

ONAGRACEÆ.

344. Epilobium montanum.

345. Epilobium roseum.

346. Epilobium tetragonum.

347. Epilobium palustre.

ONAGRACEÆ 83

348. Epilobium alsinefolium.

349. Epilobium alpinum.

350. Œnothera biennis.

351. Ludwigia palustris.

LYTHRARIEÆ.

352. Circæa lutetiana.

353. Circæa alpina.

354. Lythrum Salicaria.

355. Lythrum hyssopifolium.

CRASSULACEÆ.

356. Peplis Portula.

357. Bryonia dioica.

358. Tillæa muscosa.

359. Cotyledon Umbilicus.

360. Sedum Rhodiola.

CRASSULACEÆ.

361. Sedum Telephium.

362. Sedum anglicum.

363. Sedum dasyphyllum.

364. Sedum album.

CRASSULACEÆ.

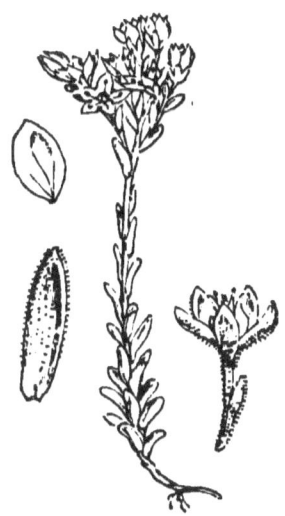

365. Sedum villosum.

366. Sedum acre.

367. Sedum sexangulare.

368. Sedum rupestre.

369. Sempervivum tectorum.

370. Ribes Grossularia.

371. Ribes rubrum.

372. Ribes alpinum.

SAXIFRAGACEÆ.

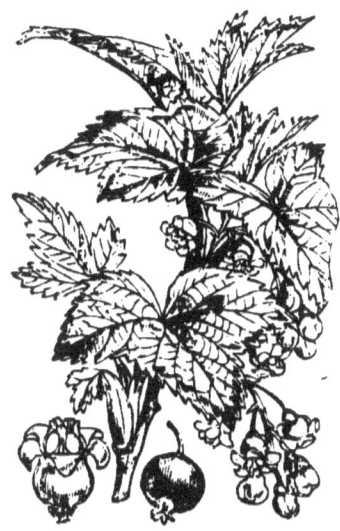

373. Ribes nigrum.

375. Saxifraga aizoides.

374. Saxifraga oppositifolia.

376. Saxifraga Hirculus.

SAXIFRAGACEÆ.

377. Saxifraga hypnoides.

379. Saxifraga granulata.

378. Saxifraga cæspitosa.

380. Saxifraga cernua.

SAXIFRAGACEÆ.

381. Saxifraga rivularis.

382. Saxifraga tridactylites.

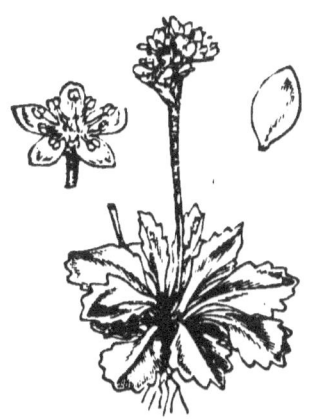

383. Saxifraga nivalis.

384. Saxifraga stellaris.

SAXIFRAGACEÆ.

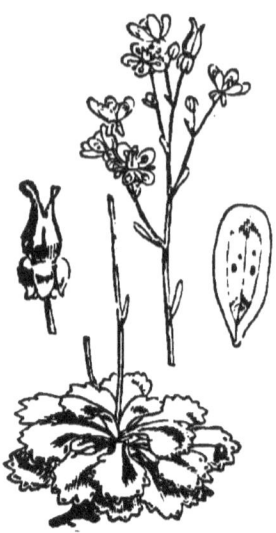

385. Saxifraga umbrosa.

386. Saxifraga Geum.

387. Chrysosplenium oppositifolium.

388. Chrysosplenium alternifolium.

DROSERACEÆ

389. Parnassia palustris

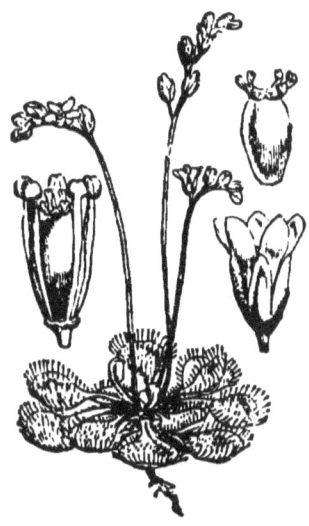

390. Drosera rotundifolia.

391. Drosera longifolia.

392. Drosera anglica.

HALORAGEÆ.

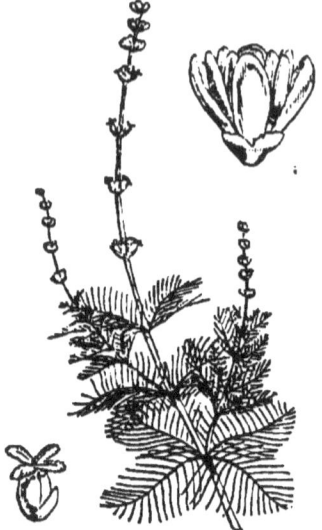
393. Myriophyllum spicatum.

394. Myriophyllum verticillatum.

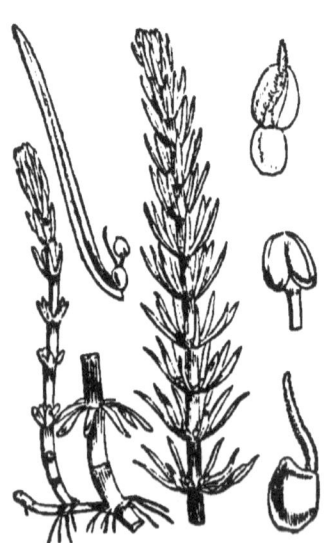
395. Hippuris vulgaris.

396. Hydrocotyle vulgaris.

UMBELLIFERÆ.

397. Sanicula europæa.

399. Eryngium maritimum.

398. Astrantia major.

400. Eryngium campestre.

UMBELLIFERÆ.

401. Cicuta virosa.

402. Apium graveolens.

403. Apium nodiflorum.

404. Apium inundatum.

UMBELLIFERÆ.

405. Sison Amomum.

406. Trinia vulgaris.

407. Ægopodium Podagraria.

408. Carum Petroselinum.

H

UMBELLIFERÆ.

409. Carum segetum.

410. Carum verticillatum.

411. Carum Carvi.

412. Carum Bulbocastanum.

413. Sium latifolium.

414. Sium angustifolium.

415. Pimpinella Saxifraga.

416. Pimpinella magna.

UMBELLIFERÆ.

417. Bupleurum rotundifolium

418. Bupleurum aristatum.

419. Bupleurum tenuissimum.

420. Bupleurum falcatum.

UMBELLIFERÆ. 101

421. Œnanthe fistulosa.

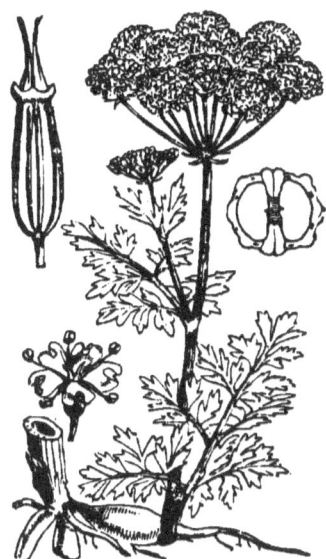

423. Œnanthe crocata.

422 Œnanthe pimpinelloides.

424. Œnanthe Phellandrium.

425. Æthusa Cynapium.

427. Seseli Libanotis.

426. Fœniculum vulgare.

428. Ligusticum scoticum.

UMBELLIFERÆ.

429. Silaus pratensis.

430. Meum athamanticum.

431. Chrithmum maritimum.

432. Angelica sylvestris.

UMBELLIFERÆ.

433. Peucedanum officinale.

435. Peucedanum Ostruthium.

434. Peucedanum palustre.

436. Pastinaca sativa.

UMBELLIFERÆ.

437. Heracleum Sphondylium.

439. Scandix Pecten.

438. Tordylium maximum.

440. Myrrhis odorata.

441. Conopodium denudatum.

443. Chærophyllum sylvestre.

442. Chærophyllum temulum.

444. Chærophyllum Anthriscus.

UMBELLIFERÆ.

445. Caucalis nodosa.

447. Caucalis arvensis.

446. Caucalis Anthriscus.

448. Caucalis daucoides.

449. Caucalis latifolia.

450. Daucus Carota.

451. Conium maculatum.

452. Physospermum cornubiense.

LORANTHACEÆ.

453. Smyrnium Olusatrum.

454. Coriandrum sativum.

455. Hedera Helix.

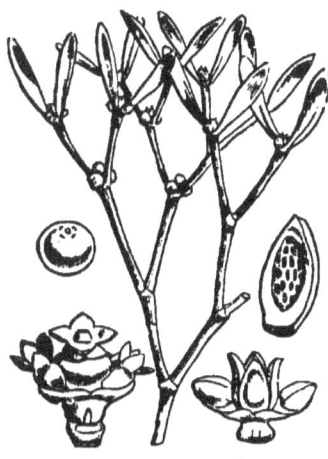

456. Viscum album.

CORNACEÆ.

457. Cornus suecica.

458. Cornus sanguinea.

459. Adoxa Moschatellina.

460. Sambucus nigra.

CAPRIFOLIACEÆ.

461. Sambucus Ebulus

462. Viburnum Lantana.

463. Viburnum Opulus.

464. Lonicera Periclymenum.

CAPRIFOLIACEÆ.

465. Lonicera Caprifolium.

466. Lonicera Xylosteum.

467. Linnæa borealis

468. Rubia peregrina.

STELLATÆ. 113

469. Galium Cruciata.

470 Galium verum.

471. Galium palustre.

472. Galium uliginosum.

STELLATÆ.

473. Galium saxatile.

474. Galium Mollugo.

475. Galium anglicum.

476. Galium boreale.

STELLATÆ. 115

477. Galium Aparine.

478. Galium tricorne.

479. Asperula odorata.

480. Asperula cynanchica.

481. Sherardia arvensis.

483. Valeriana dioica.

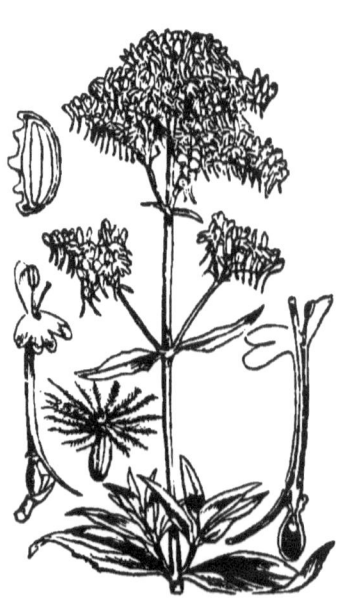

482. Centranthus ruber.

484. Valeriana officinalis.

VALERIANEÆ.

485. Valeriana pyrenaica.

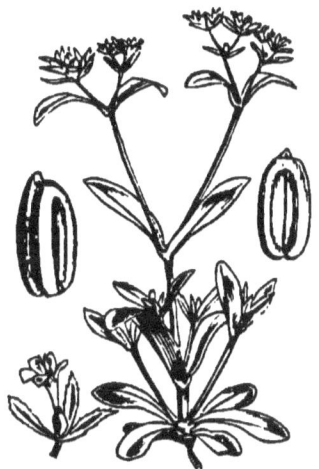

487. Valerianella carinata.

486. Valerianella olitoria.

488. Valerianella Auricula.

489. Valerianella dentata.

490. Dipsacus sylvestris.

491. Dipsacus pilosus.

492. Scabiosa succisa.

COMPOSITÆ.

493. Scabiosa Columbaria.

494. Scabiosa arvensis.

495. Eupatorium cannabinum.

496. Aster Tripolium.

COMPOSITÆ.

497. Aster Linosyris.

499. Erigeron alpinus.

498. Erigeron acris.

500. Erigeron canadensis.

COMPOSITÆ.

501. Solidaga Virga-aurea.

502. Bellis perennis.

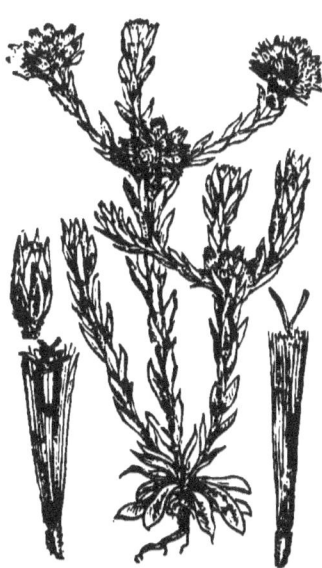

503. Filago Germanica

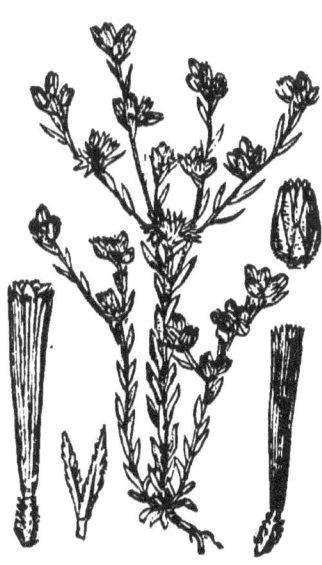

504. Filago minima.

COMPOSITÆ.

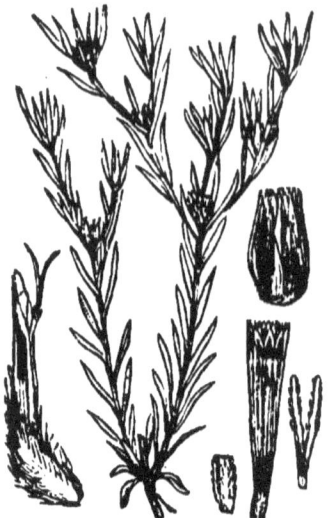

505. Filago gallica.

507. Gnaphalium sylvaticum.

506. Gnaphalium luteo-album.

508. Gnaphalium supinum.

COMPOSITÆ.

509. Gnaphalium uliginosum.

510. Antennaria dioica.

511. Antennaria margaritacea.

512. Inula Helenium.

COMPOSITÆ.

513. Inula salicina.

514. Inula crithmoides.

515. Inula Conyza.

516. Inula dysenterica.

COMPOSITÆ.

517 Inula Pulicaria.

518. Xanthium Strumarium.

519. Bidens cernua.

520. Bidens tripartita.

COMPOSITÆ.

521. Chrysanthemum Leucanthemum.

522. Chrysanthemum segetum.

523. Chrysanthemum Parthenium.

524. Matricaria inodora.

COMPOSITÆ.

525. Matricaria Chamomilla.

526. Anthemis Cotula.

527. Anthemis arvensis.

528. Anthemis nobilis.

COMPOSITÆ.

529. Anthemis tinctoria.

530. Achillea Ptarmica.

531. Achillea Millefolium.

532. Diotis maritima.

COMPOSITÆ.

533. Tanacetum vulgare.

534. Artemisia campestris.

535. Artemisia maritima.

536. Artemisia vulgaris.

K

COMPOSITÆ.

537. Artemisia Absinthium.

538. Tussilago Farfara.

539. Tussilago Petasites.

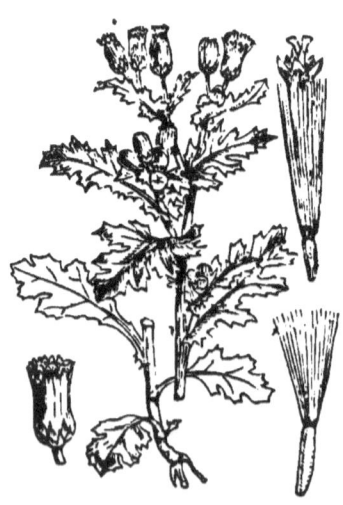

540. Senecio vulgaris.

 541. Senecio viscosus.

 542. Senecio sylvaticus.

 543. Senecio squalidus.

 544. Senecio aquaticus.

132 COMPOSITÆ.

545. Senecio Jacobæa.

546. Senecio erucifolius.

547. Senecio paludosus.

548. Senecio saracenicus.

COMPOSITÆ. 133

549. Senecio palustris.

550. Senecio campestris.

551. Doronicum Pardalianches.

552. Doronicum plantagineum.

COMPOSITÆ.

553. Arctium Lappa.

554. Serratula tinctoria.

555. Saussurea alpina.

556. Carduus Marianus.

COMPOSITÆ. 135

557. Carduus nutans.

558. Carduus acanthoides.

559. Carduus pycnocephalus.

560. Carduus lanceolatus.

COMPOSITÆ.

561. Carduus palustris.

562. Carduus arvensis.

563. Carduus eriophorus.

564. Carduus heterophyllus.

COMPOSITÆ. 137

565. Carduus tuberosus.

566. Carduus pratensis.

567. Carduus acaulis.

568. Onopordon Acanthium.

COMPOSITÆ.

569. Carlina vulgaris.

570. Centaurea nigra.

571. Centaurea Scabiosa.

572. Centaurea Cyanus.

COMPOSITÆ.

573. Centaurea aspera.

574. Centaurea Calcitrapa.

575. Centaurea solstitialis. 576. Tragopogon pratensis.

COMPOSITÆ.

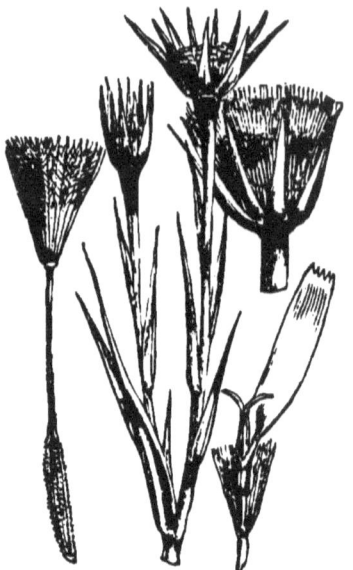

577. Tragopogon porrifolius.

578. Helminthia echioides.

579. Picris hieracioides.

580. Leontodon hispidus.

COMPOSITÆ.

581. Leontodon autumnalis.

582. Leontodon hirtus.

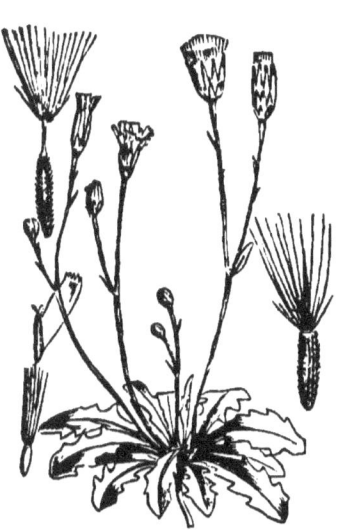

583. Hypochœris glabra.

584. Hypochœris radicata.

COMPOSITÆ.

585. Hypochœris maculata.

586. Lactuca muralis.

587. Lactuca Scariola.

588. Lactuca saligna.

COMPOSITÆ. 143

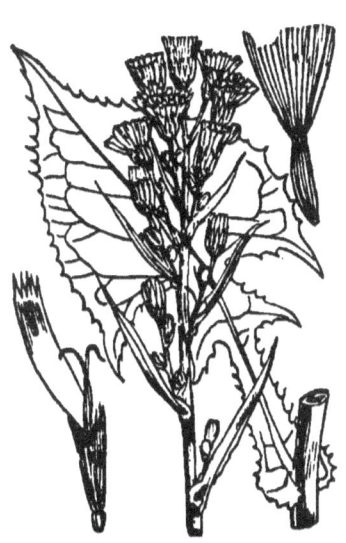

589. Lactuca alpina.

590. Sonchus arvensis.

591. Sonchus palustris.

592. Sonchus oleraceus.

COMPOSITÆ.

593. Taraxacum Dens-leonis.

594. Crepis taraxacifolia.

595. Crepis fœtida.

596. Crepis virens.

COMPOSITÆ.

597. Crepis biennis.

599. Crepis paludosa.

598. Crepis hieracioides.

600. Hieracium Pilosella.

L

COMPOSITÆ.

601. Hieracium alpinum.

602. Hieracium murorum.

603. Hieracium cerinthoides.

604. Hieracium umbellatum.

COMPOSITÆ.

605. Hieracium sabaudum.

606. Hieracium prenanthoides.

607. Cichorium Intybus.

608. Arnoseris pusilla.

CAMPANULACEÆ.

609. Lapsana communis.

611. Lobelia urens.

610. Lobelia Dortmanna.

612. Jasione montana.

CAMPANULACEÆ.

613. Phyteuma orbiculare.

614. Phyteuma spicatum.

615. Campanula glomerata.

616. Campanula Trachelium.

CAMPANULACEÆ.

617. Campanula latifolia.

618. Campanula rapunculoides.

619. Campanula Rapunculus.

620. Campanula patula.

ERICACEÆ.

621. Campanula rotundifolia.

623. Campanula hybrida.

622. Campanula hederacea.

624. Vaccinium Myrtillus.

ERICACEÆ.

625. Vaccinium uliginosum.

626. Vaccinium Vitis-idæa.

627. Vaccinium Oxycoccos.

628. Arbutus Unedo.

ERICACEÆ. 153

629. Arctostaphylos Uva-ursi.

631. Andromeda polifolia.

630. Arctostaphylos alpina.

632. Loiseleuria procumbens.

ERICACEÆ.

633. Menziesia polifolia.

634. Menziesia cærulea.

635. Erica cinerea.

636. Erica Tetralix.

ERICACEÆ. 155

637. Erica ciliaris.

638. Erica carnea.

639. Erica vagans.

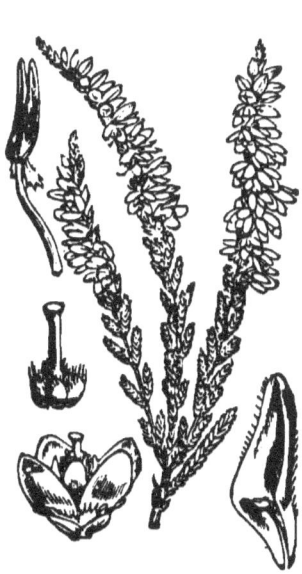

640. Calluna vulgaris.

ERICACEÆ.

641. Pyrola uniflora.

642. Pyrola rotundifolia.

643. Pyrola media.

644. Pyrola minor.

PRIMULACEÆ.

645. Pyrola secunda.

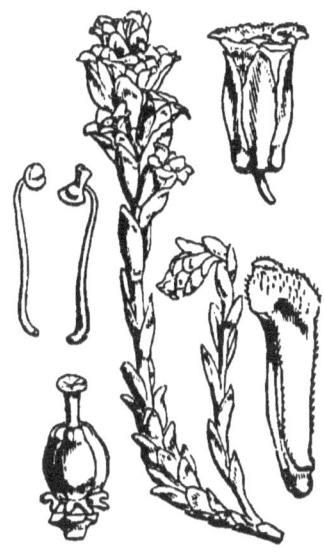

646. Monotropa Hypopitys.

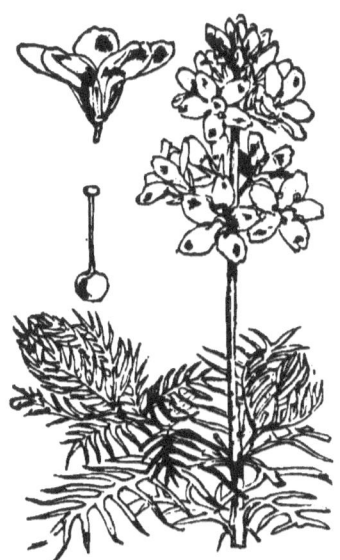

647. Hottonia palustris.

648. Primula vulgaris.

PRIMULACEÆ.

649. Primula veris.

650. Primula farinosa.

651. Cyclamen europæum.

652. Lysimachia vulgaris.

PRIMULACEÆ.

653. Lysimachia thyrsiflora.

655. Lysimachia nemorum.

654. Lysimachia Nummularia.

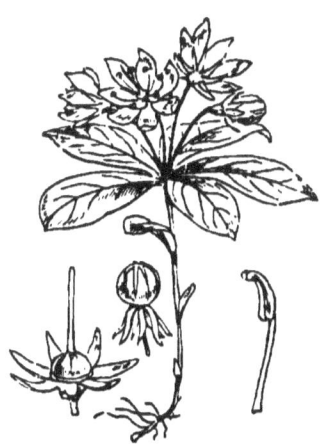

656. Trientalis europæa.

PRIMULACEÆ.

657. Glaux maritima.

658. Anagallis arvensis.

659. Anagallis tenella.

660. Centunculus minimus.

661. Samolus Valerandi.

LENTIBULACEÆ. 161

662. Pinguicula vulgaris.

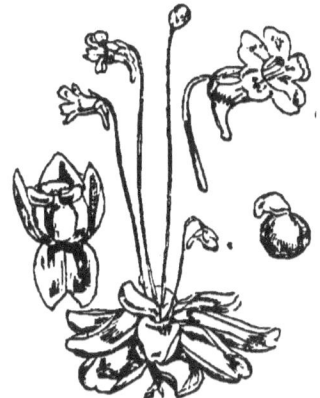

664. Pinguicula lusitanica.

663. Pinguicula alpina.

665. Utricularia vulgaris.

M

OLEACEÆ.

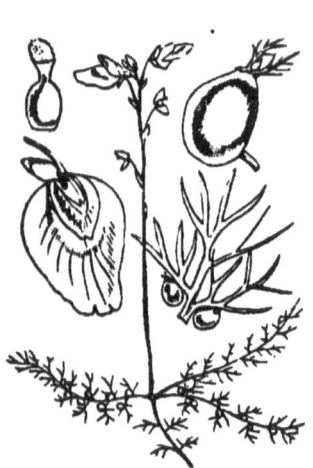

666. Utricularia minor.

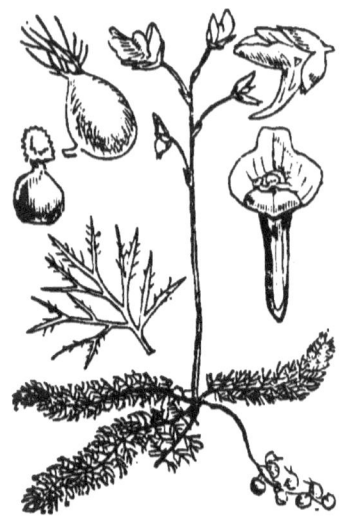

667. Utricularia intermedia.

668. Fraxinus excelsior.

669. Ligustrum vulgare.

GENTIANACEÆ. 163

670. Vinca major.

671. Vinca minor.

672. Cicendia filiformis.

674. Erythræa Centaurium.

673. Cicendia pusilla.

675. Gentiana Pneumonanthe.   676. Gentiana verna.

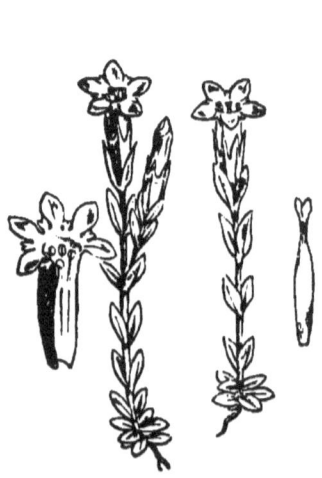

677. Gentiana nivalis.   678. Gentiana Amarella.

GENTIANACEÆ.

679. Gentiana campestris.

681. Menyanthes trifoliata.

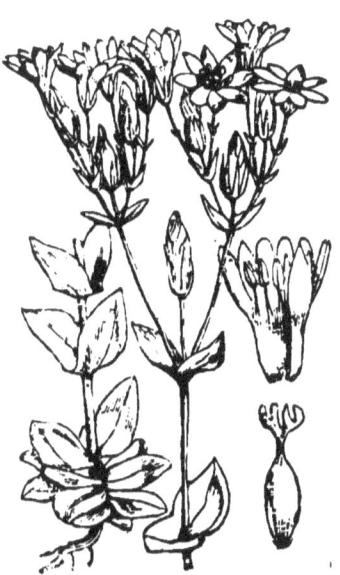

680. Chlora perfoliata.

682. Limnanthemum nymphæoides.

POLEMONIACEÆ.

683. Polemonium cæruleum.

684. Convolvulus arvensis.

685. Convolvulus sepium.

686. Convolvulus Soldanella.

CONVOLVULACEÆ.

687. Cuscuta europæa.

688. Cuscuta Epilinum.

689. Cuscuta Epithymum.

690   Echium vulgare.

691.   Echium plantagineum.

BORAGINEÆ.

 692. Pulmonaria officinalis.

 693. Mertensia maritima.

 694. Lithospermum arvense.

 695. Lithospermum officinale.

BORAGINEÆ.

696. Lithospermum purpureo-cæruleum.

697. Myosotis palustris.

698. Myosotis sylvatica.

699. Myosotis arvensis.

BORAGINEÆ.

700. Myosotis collina.

701. Myosotis versicolor.

702. Anchusa officinalis.

703. Anchusa sempervirens.

BORAGINEÆ.

704. Lycopsis arvensis.

705. Symphytum officinale.

706. Symphytum tuberosum.

707. Borago officinalis.

172 BORAGINEÆ.

708. Asperugo procumbens.

710. Cynoglossum montanum.

709. Cynoglossum officinale.

711. Datura Stramonium.

SOLANACEÆ.

712. Hyoscyamus niger.

713. Solanum Dulcamara.

714. Solanum nigrum.

715. Atropa Belladonna.

OROBANCHACEÆ.

716. Orobanche major.

717. Orobanche caryophyllacea.

718. Orobanche rubra.

719. Orobanche elatior.

OROBANCHACEÆ.

720. Orobanche minor.

721. Orobanche cærulea.

722. Orobanche ramosa.

723. Lathræa squamaria.

SCROPHULARINEÆ.

724. Verbascum Thapsus.

725. Verbascum Blattaria.

726. Verbascum virgatum.

727. Verbascum nigrum.

SCROPHULARINEÆ.

728. Verbascum Lychnitis.

729. Verbascum pulverulentum.

730. Antirrhinum majus.

731. Antirrhinum Orontium.

SCROPHULARINEÆ.

372. Linaria vulgaris.

733. Linaria repens.

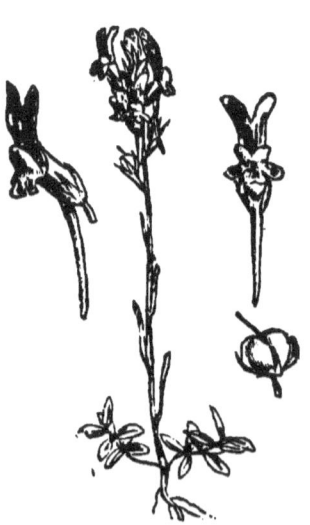

734. Linaria Pelisseriana.

735. Linaria supina.

SCROPHULARINEÆ. 179

736. Linaria minor.

738. Linaria spuria.

737. Linaria Cymbalaria.

739. Linaria Elatine.

740. Scrophularia nodosa.

741. Scrophularia aquatica.

742. Scrophularia Scorodonia.

743. Scrophularia vernalis.

744. Mimulus luteus.

SCROPHULARINEÆ.

745. Limosella aquatica.

746. Sibthorpia europæa.

747. Digitalis purpurea.

748. Veronica spicata.

SCROPHULARINEÆ.

749. Veronica saxatilis.

750. Veronica alpina.

751. Veronica serpyllifolia.

752. Veronica officinalis.

SCROPHULARINEÆ.

753. Veronica Anagallis.

755. Veronica scutellata.

754. Veronica Beccabunga.

756. Veronica montana.

SCROPHULARINEÆ.

757. Veronica Chamædrys.

758. Veronica hederæfolia.

759. Veronica agrestis.

760. Veronica Buxbaumii.

761. Veronica arvensis.

SCROPHULARINEÆ. 185

762. Veronica verna.

763. Veronica triphyllos.

764. Bartsia alpina.

765. Bartsia viscosa.

SCROPHULARINEÆ.

766. Bartsia Odontites.

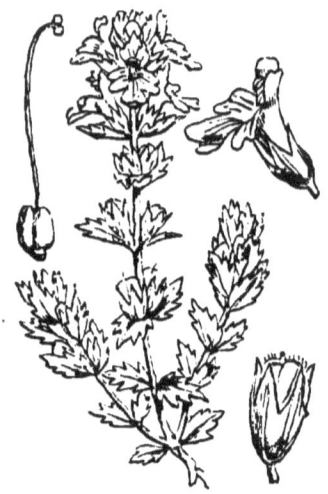

767. Euphrasia officinalis.

768. Rhinanthus Crista-galli.

769. Pedicularis palustris.

SCROPHULARINEÆ.

770. Pedicularis sylvatica.

771. Melampyrum cristatum.

772. Melampyrum arvense.

773. Melampyrum pratense.

LABIATÆ.

774. Melampyrum sylvaticum.

775. Salvia pratensis.

776. Salvia Verbenaca.

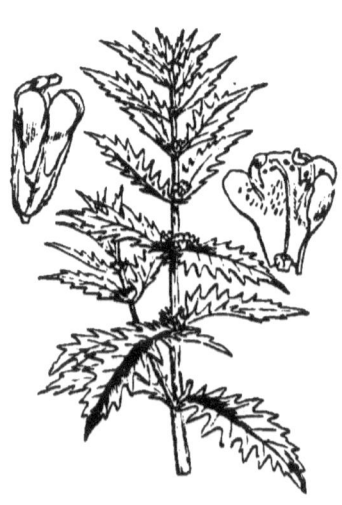

777. Lycopus europæus.

778. Mentha sylvestris.

779. Mentha rotundifolia.

780. Mentha viridis.

781. Mentha piperita.

782. Mentha aquatica.

783. Mentha sativa.

784. Mentha arvensis.

785. Mentha Pulegium.

LABIATÆ.

786. Thymus Serpyllum.

787. Origanum vulgare.

788. Calamintha Acinos.

789. Calamintha officinalis.

LABIATÆ.

790. Calamintha Clinopodium.

791. Nepeta Glechoma.

792. Nepeta Cataria.

793. Prunella vulgaris.

LABIATÆ.

794. Scutellaria galericulata.

795. Scutellaria minor.

796. Melittis Melissophyllum.

797. Marrubium vulgare.

o

194   LABIATÆ.

798. Stachys Betonica.

799. Stachys germanica.

800. Stachys sylvatica

801. Stachys palustris.

LABIATÆ. 195

802. Stachys arvensis.

803. Galeopsis Ladanum.

804. Galeopsis ochroleuca.

805. Galeopsis Tetrahit.

o 2

LABIATÆ.

806. Ballota nigra.

807. Leonurus Cardiaca.

808. Lamium amplexicaule.

809. Lamium purpureum.

LABIATÆ.

810. Lamium album.

811. Lamium maculatum.

812. Lamium Galeobdolon.

813. Teucrium Scorodonia.

LABIATÆ.

814. Teucrium Scordium.

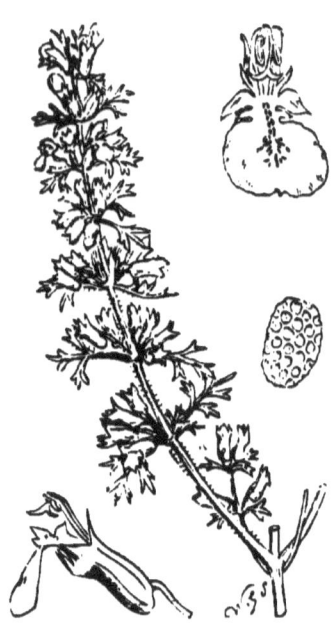

815. Teucrium Botrys.

816. Teucrium Chamædrys.

817. Ajuga reptans.

VERBINACEÆ.

818. Ajuga genevensis.

819. Ajuga Chamæpitys.

820. Verbena officinalis.

821. Statice Limonium.

PLUMBAGINEÆ.

822. Statice auriculæfolia.

823. Statice reticulata.

824. Armeria vulgaris.

825. Armeria plantaginea.

PLANTAGINEÆ.

826. Plantago major.

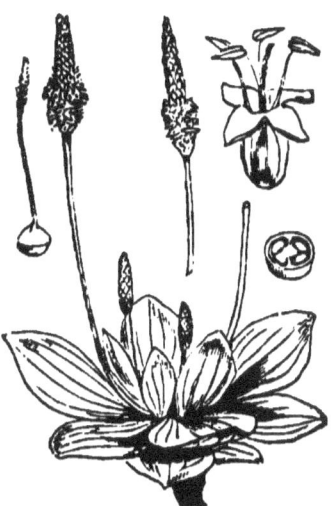

827. Plantago media.

828. Plantago lanceolata.

829. Plantago maritima.

ILLECEBRACEÆ.

830. Plantago Coronopus.

833. Herniaria glabra.

831. Littorella lacustris.

834. Illecebrum verticillatum.

832. Corrigiola littoralis.

835. Scleranthus annuus.

CHENOPODIACEÆ.

36. Scleranthus perennis.

837. Salicornia herbacea.

838. Suæda fruticosa.

839. Suæda maritima.

CHENOPODIACEÆ.

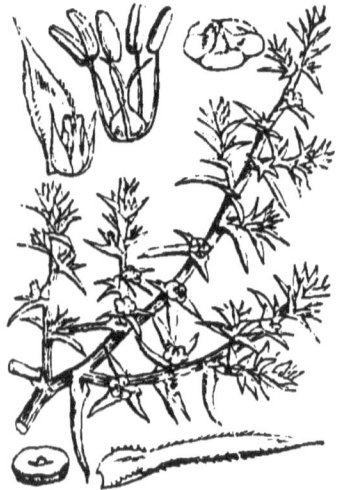

840. Salsola Kali.

841. Chenopodium Vulvaria.

842. Chenopodium polyspermum.

843. Chenopodium album.

CHENOPODIACEÆ.

844. Chenopodium glaucum.

845. Chenopodium rubrum.

846. Chenopodium urbicum.

847. Chenopodium murale.

CHENOPODIACEÆ.

848. Chenopodium hybridum.

849. Chenopodium Bonus-Henricus.

850. Beta maritima.

851. Atriplex portulacoides.

852. Atriplex pedunculata.

853. Atriplex hortensis.

854. Atriplex patula.

855. Atriplex rosea.

POLYGONACEÆ.

856. Rumex aquaticus.

857. Rumex crispus.

858. Rumex obtusifolius.

859. Rumex Hydrolapathum.

POLYGONACEÆ.

860. Rumex conglomeratus.

861. Rumex sanguineus.

862. Rumex pulcher.

863. Rumex maritimus.

POLYGONACFÆ.

864. Rumex Acetosa.

865. Rumex Acetosella.

866. Oxyria reniformis.

867. Polygonum aviculare.

POLYGONACEÆ.

868. Polygonum maritimum.   869. Polygonum Convolvulus.

870. Polygonum dumetorum.   871. Polygonum viviparum.

POLYGONACEÆ.

872. Polygonum Bistorta.

873. Polygonum amphibium.

874. Polygonum Persicaria.

875. Polygonum lapathifolium.

THYMELEACEÆ.

876. Polygonum Hydropiper.

877. Polygonum minus.

878. Daphne Mezereum.

879. Daphne Laureola.

ELÆAGNACEÆ.

880. Hippophæ rhamnoides.

881. Thesium linophyllum.

882. Asarum europæum.

883. Euphorbia Peplis.

EUPHORBIACEÆ.

884. Euphorbia Helioscopia.

Euphorbia platyphyllos.

886. Euphorbia hiberna.

887. Euphorbia pilosa.

EUPHORBIACEÆ.

888. Euphorbia Peplus.

889. Euphorbia exigua.

890. Euphorbia Lathyris.

891. Euphorbia segetalis.

892. Euphorbia Paralias.

893. Euphorbia Esula.

894. Euphorbia amygdaloides.

895. Mercurialis perennis.

218   EMPETRACEÆ.

896. Mercurialis annua.   897. Buxus sempervirens.

898. Empetrum nigrum.   899. Ceratophyllum demersum.

URTICACEÆ.

900. Callitriche aquatica.

901. Urtica urens.

902. Urtica pilulifera.

903. Urtica dioica.

ULMACEÆ.

904. Parietaria officinalis.

905. Humulus Lupulus.

906. Ulmus montana.

907. Ulmus campestris.

AMENTACEÆ.

908. Myrica Gale.

909. Alnus glutinosa.

910. Betula alba.

911. Betula nana.

AMENTACEÆ.

912. Carpinus Betulus.

913. Corylus Avellana.

914. Fagus sylvatica.

915. Quercus Robur.

AMENTACEÆ. 223

916. Salix pentandra.   917. Salix fragilis.

918. Salix alba.   919. Salix amygdalina.

AMENTACEÆ.

920. Salix purpurea.

921. Salix viminalis.

922. Salix Caprea.

923. Salix aurita.

AMENTACEÆ.

924. Salix phylicifolia.

925. Salix repens.

926. Salix Lapponum.

927. Salix lanata.

Q

AMENTACEÆ.

928. Salix Myrsinites.

929. Salix reticulata.

930. Salix herbacea.

931. Populus alba.

932. Populus tremula.

CONIFERÆ.

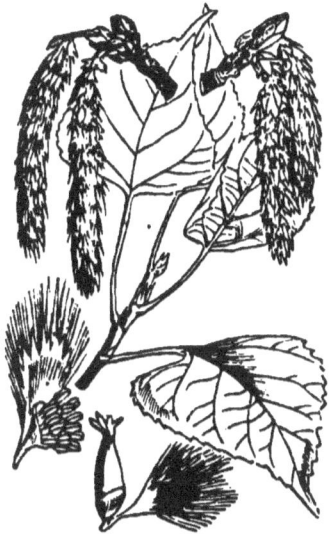

933. Populus nigra.

934. Pinus sylvestris.

935 Juniperus communis.

936. Taxus baccata.

TYPHACEÆ.

937. Typha latifolia.

938. Typha angustifolia.

939. Sparganium ramosum.

940. Sparganium simplex.

AROIDEÆ.

941. Sparganium minimum.

942. Arum maculatum.

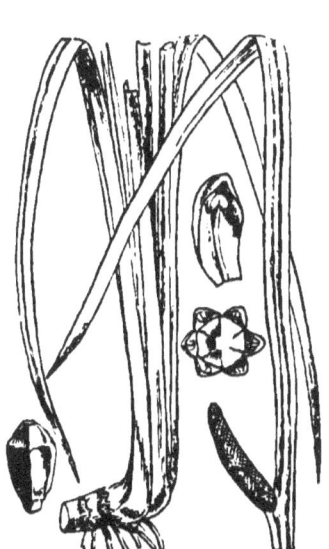

943. Acorus Calamus.

944. Lemna trisulca.

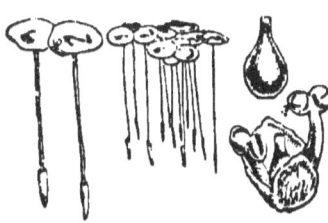

945. Lemna minor.

LEMNACEÆ.

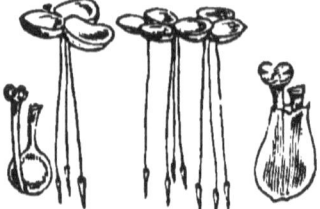

946. Lemna gibba.

947. Lemna polyrrhiza.

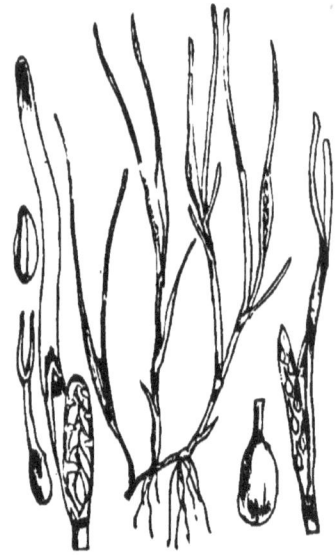

950. Zostera nana.

948. Lemna arrhiza.

949. Zostera marina.

951. Naias flexilis.

NAIADEÆ. 231

952. Naias marina.

953. Naias gramiinea.

954. Zannichellia palustris.

955. Ruppia maritima.

232   NAIADEÆ.

956. Potamogeton natans.   957. Potamogeton heterophyllus.

958. Potamogeton lucens.   959. Potamogeton prælongus.

960. Potamogeton perfoliatus.

961. Potamogeton crispus.

962. Potamogeton densus.

963. Potamogeton obtusifolius.

NALADEÆ.

964. Potamogeton acutifolius.

965. Potamogeton pusillus.

966. Potamogeton pectinatus.

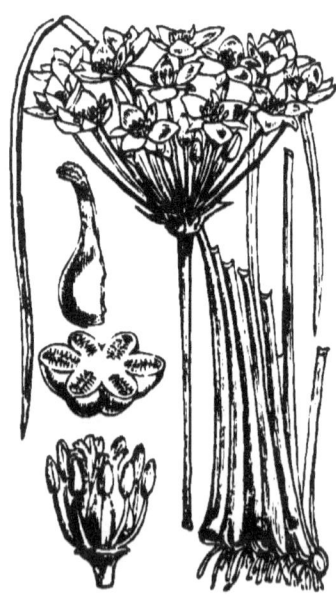

967. Butomus umbellatus.

ALISMACEÆ.

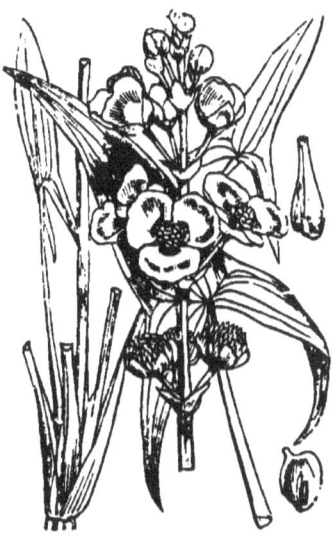

968. Sagittaria sagittifolia.

969. Alisma Plantago.

970. Alisma ranunculoides.

971. Alisma natans.

ALISMACEÆ.

972. Damasonium stellatum.

973. Scheuchzeria palustris.

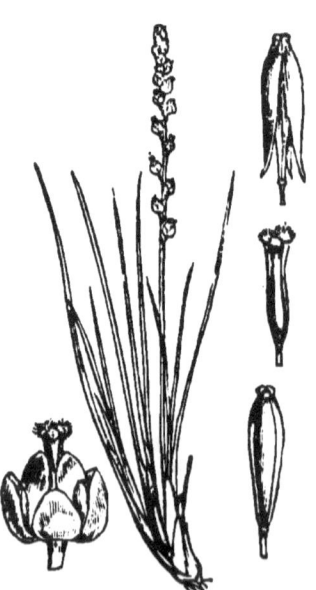

974. Triglochin palustre.

975. Triglochin maritimum.

HYDROCHARIDEÆ.

976. Elodea canadensis.

977. Hydrocharis Morsus-ranæ.

978. Stratiotes aloides.

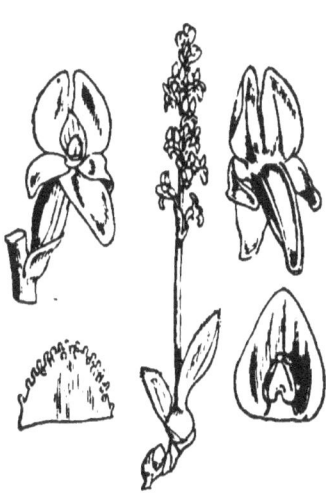

979. Malaxis paludosa.

ORCHIDACEÆ.

980. Liparis Loeselii.

981. Corallorhiza innata.

982. Epipactis latifolia.

983. Epipactis palustris.

984. Cephalanthera grandiflora.

985. Cephalanthera ensifolia.

986. Cephalanthera rubra.

987. Listera ovata.

240 ORCHIDACEÆ.

988. Listera cordata.

989. Neottia Nidus-avis

990. Epipogum aphyllum.

991. Spiranthes autumnalis.

ORCHIDACEÆ.

992. Spiranthes æstivalis.

993. Spiranthes Romazoviana.

994. Goodyera repens.

995. Orchis Morio

R

ORCHIDACEÆ.

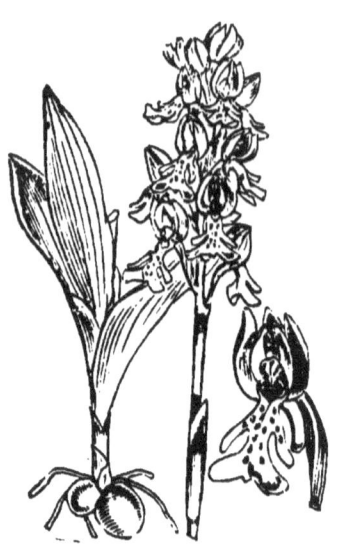

996. Orchis militaris.

997. Orchis ustulata.

998. Orchis mascula.

999. Orchis laxiflora.

ORCHIDACEÆ. 243

1000 Orchis maculata.

1001. Orchis latifolia.

1002. Orchis hircina.

1003. Orchis pyramidalis.

1004. Habenaria bifolia.

1005. Habenaria conopsea.

1006. Habenaria intacta.

1007. Habenaria albida.

ORCHIDACEÆ.

1008. Habenaria viridis.

1009. Aceras anthropophora.

1010. Herminium Monorchis.

1011. Ophrys apifera.

ORCHIDACEÆ.

1012. Ophrys aranifera.

1013. Ophrys mucifera.

1014. Cypripedium Calceolus.

1015. Iris Pseudacorus.

IRIDEÆ.

1016. Iris fœtidissima.

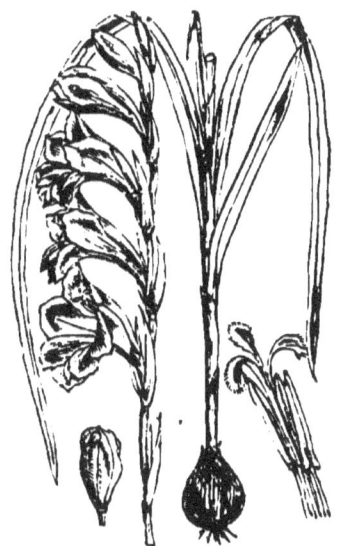

1017. Gladiolus communis.

1018. Sisyrinchum angustifolium.

1019. Romulea Columnæ.

AMARYLLIDEÆ.

1020. Crocus vernus.

1021. Crocus nudiflorus.

1022. Narcissus Pseudonarcissus.

1023. Narcissus biflorus.

DIOSCORIDEÆ.

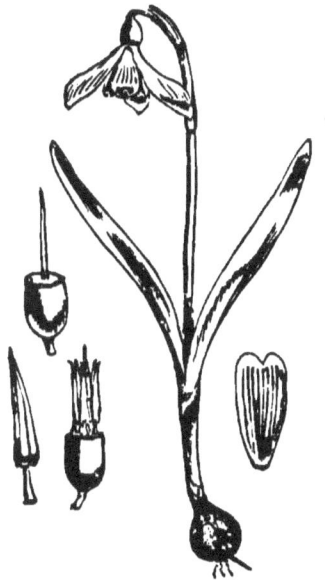

1024. Galanthus nivalis.

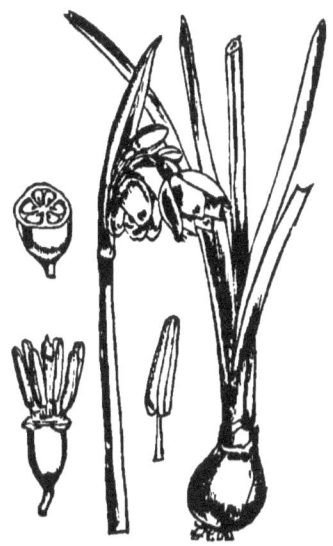

1025. Leucoium æstivum.

1026. Tamus communis.

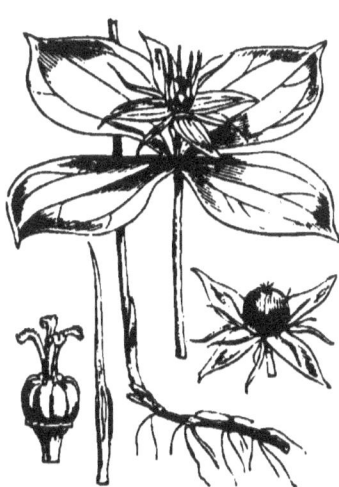

1027. Paris quadrifolia.

250　LILIACEÆ.

1028. Polygonatum verticillatum.

1029. Polygonatum multiflorum.

1030. Polygonatum officinale.

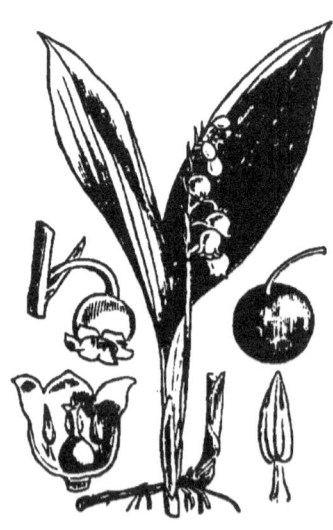

1031. Convallaria majalis.

LILIACEÆ.

1032. Maianthemum Convallaria.

1033. Asparagus officinalis.

1034. Ruscus aculeatus.

1035. Fritillaria Meleagris.

LILIACEÆ.

1036. Tulipa sylvestris.

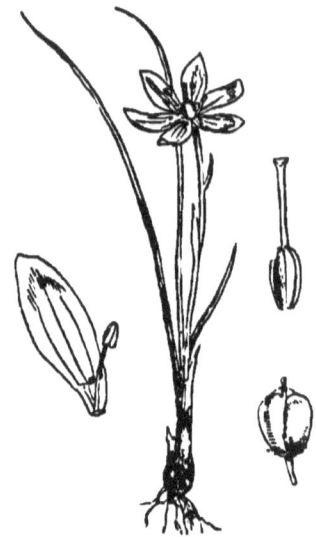

1037. Lloydia serotina.

1038. Gagea lutea.

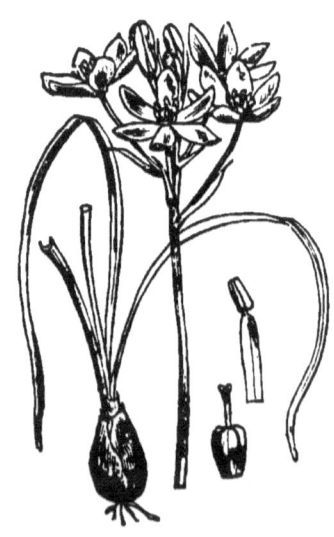

1039. Ornithogalum umbellatum.

LILIACEÆ.

1040. Ornithogalum nutans.

1041. Ornithogalum pyrenaicum.

1042. Scilla verna.

1043 Scilla autumnalis.

LILIACEÆ.

1044. Scilla nutans.

1045. Muscari racemosum.

1046. Allium Ampeloprasum.

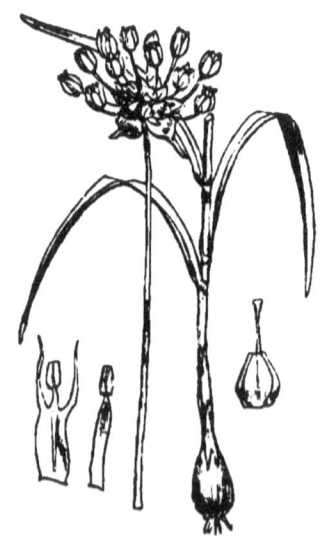

1047. Allium Scorodoprasum.

LILIACEÆ. 255

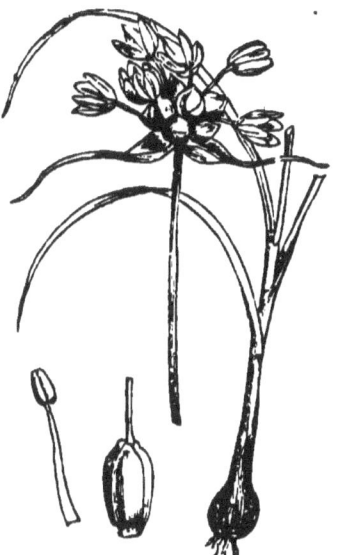

1048. Allium oleraceum.

1049 Allium Schœnoprasum.

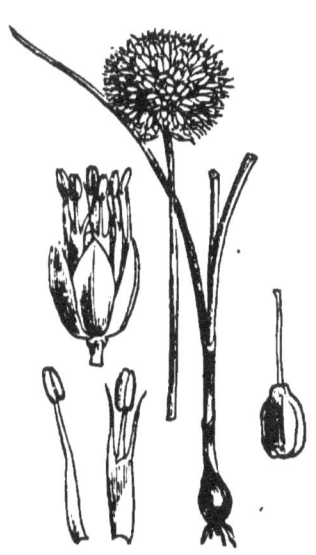

1050. Allium sphærocephalum.

1051. Allium vineale.

LILIACEÆ.

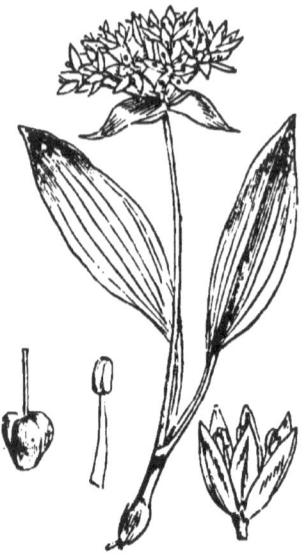

1052. Allium ursinum.

1053. Allium triquetrum.

1054. Simethis bicolor.

1055. Narthecium ossifragum.

1056. Tofieldia palustris.

1057. Colchicum autumnale.

1058. Juncus communis.

1059. Juncus glaucus.

JUNCACEÆ.

1060. Juncus filiformis.

1061. Juncus balticus.

1062. Juncus articulatus.

1063. Juncus obtusiflorus.

JUNCACEÆ.

1064. Juncus compressus.

1065. Juncus tenuis.

1066. Juncus squarrosus.

1067. Juncus bufonius.

JUNCACEÆ.

1068. Juncus pygmæus.

1069. Juncus capitatus.

1070 Juncus maritimus.

1071. Juncus acutus.

JUNCACEÆ.

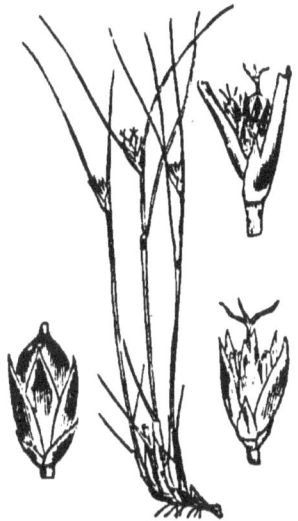

1072. Juncus trifidus

1073. Juncus castaneus.

1074. Juncus biglumis.

1075. Luzula pilosa.

JUNCACEÆ.

1076. Luzula sylvatica.

1078. Luzula campestris.

1077. Luzula arcuata.

1079. Luzula spicata.

CYPERACEÆ.

1080. Eriocaulon septangulare.

1082. Cyperus fuscus

1081. Cyperus longus.

1083. Schœnus nigricans.

CYPERACEÆ.

1084. Cladium Mariscus.

1085. Rhynchospora fusca.

1086. Rhynchospora alba.

1087. Blysmus compressus.

CYPERACEÆ.

1088. Blysmus rufus.

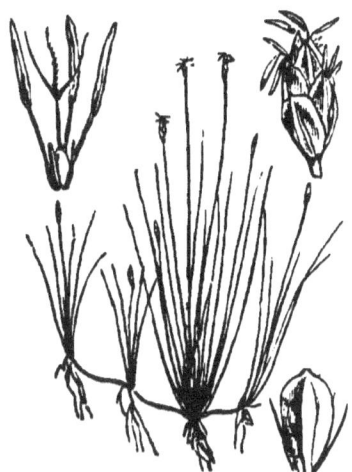

1089. Scirpus acicularis.

1090. Scirpus parvulus.

1091. Scirpus palustris.

1092. Scirpus multicaulis.

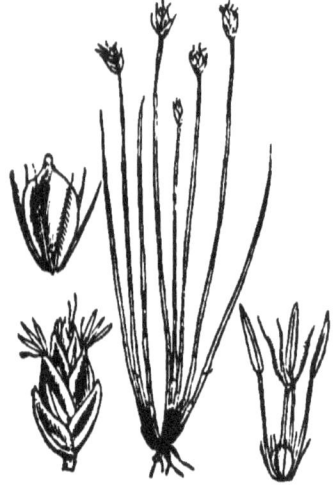

1093. Scirpus pauciflorus.

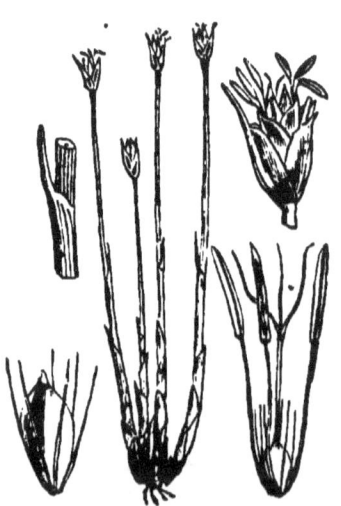

1094. Scirpus cæspitosus.

1095. Scirpus fluitans.

CYPERACEÆ.

1096. Scirpus setaceus.

1097. Scirpus Savii.

1098. Scirpus Holoschœnus.

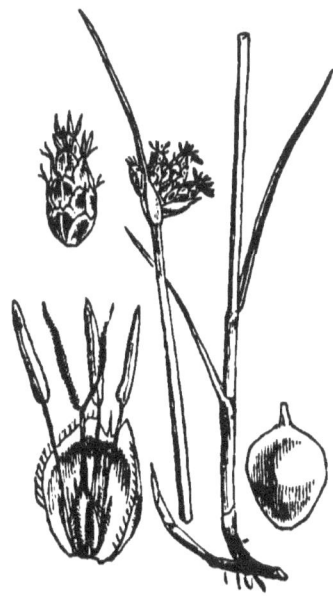

1099. Scirpus pungens.

CYPERACEÆ.

1100. Scirpus triqueter.

1101. Scirpus lacustris.

1102. Scirpus maritimus.

1103. Scirpus sylvaticus.

CYPERACEÆ. 269

1104. Eriophorum alpinum.

1105. Eriophorum vaginatum.

1106. Eriophorum polystachion

1107. Kobresia caricina.

CYPERACEÆ.

1108. Carex dioica.

1109. Carex pulicaris.

1110. Carex rupestris.

1111. Carex pauciflora.

CYPERACEÆ.

1112. Carex leporina.

1113. Carex lagopina.

1114. Carex elongata.

1115. Carex stellulata.

CYPERACEÆ.

1116. Carex canescens.

1117. Carex remota.

1118. Carex axillaris.

1119. Carex paniculata.

CYPERACEÆ. 273

1120. Carex vulpina.

1122. Carex arenaria.

1121. Carex muricata.

1123. Carex divisa.

T

CYPERACEÆ.

1124. Carex incurva.

1125. Carex saxatilis.

1126. Carex cæspitosa.

1127. Carex acuta.

CYPERACEÆ.

1128. Carex alpina.

1129. Carex Buxbaumii.

1130. Carex atrata.

1131. Carex humilis.

CYPERACEÆ.

1132. Carex digitata.

1133. Carex præcox.

1134. Carex montana.

1135. Carex pilulifera.

CYPERACEÆ.

1136. Carex tomentosa.

1137. Carex filiformis.

1138. Carex hirta.

1139. Carex pallescens.

278　　　　　　　　　CYPERACEÆ.

1140.　Carex extensa.

1141.　Carex flava.

1142.　Carex distans.

1143.　Carex punctata.

CYPERACEÆ.

1144. Carex panicea

1145. Carex capillaris.

1146. Carex limosa.

1147 Carex glauca.

1148. Carex sylvatica.

1149. Carex strigosa.

1150. Carex Pseudocyperus.

1151. Carex pendula.

GRAMINEÆ.

1152. Carex ampullacea.

1153. Carex vesicaria.

1154. Carex paludosa

1155. Leersia oryzoides.

1156. Milium effusum.

1157. Panicum sanguinale.

1158. Panicum glabrum.

1159. Panicum verticillatum.

GRAMINEÆ. 283

1160. Panicum glaucum.

1161. Panicum viride.

1162. Panicum Crus-galli.

1163. Hierochloe borealis.

GRAMINEÆ.

1164. Anthoxanthum odoratum.

1165. Phalaris canariensis.

1166. Digraphis arundinacea.

1167. Phleum pratense.

GRAMINEÆ.

1168   Phleum alpinum.

1169.   Phleum Bœhmeri.

1170.   Phleum asperum.

1171.   Phleum arenarium.

GRAMINEÆ.

1172. Alopecurus agrestis.

1173. Alopecurus pratensis.

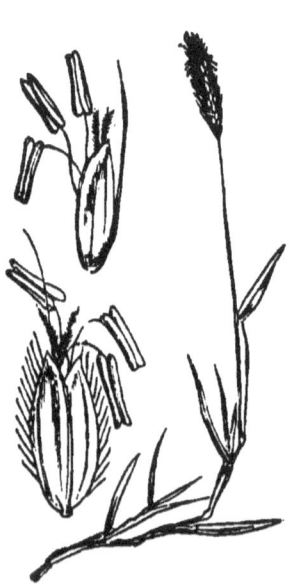

1174. Alopecurus geniculatus.

1175. Alopecurus alpinus.

GRAMINEÆ.

1176. Chamagrostis minima.

1177. Lagurus ovatus

1178. Polypogon monspeliensis.

1179. Polypogon littoralis.

GRAMINEÆ.

1180. Agrostis alba.

1181. Agrostis canina.

1182. Agrostis cetacea.

1183. Agrostis Spica-venti.

GRAMINEÆ.

1184. Gastridium lendigerum.

1185. Psamma arenaria.

1186 Calamagrostis Epigeios.

1187. Calamagrostis lanceolata

GRAMINEÆ.

1188. Calamagrostis stricta.

1189. Aira cæspitosa.

1190. Aira flexuosa.

1191. Aira canescens.

GRAMINEÆ.

1192. Aira præcox.

1193. Aira caryophyllea.

1194. Avena fatua.

1195. Avena pratensis.

GRAMINEÆ.

1196. Avena flavescens.

1197. Arrhenatherum avenaceum.

1198. Holcus lanatus.

1199. Holcus mollis.

GRAMINEÆ.

1200. Cynodon Dactylon.

1201. Spartina stricta.

1202. Lepturus incurvatus.

1203. Nardus stricta.

GRAMINEÆ.

1204. Elymus arenarius.

1205. Hordeum sylvaticum.

1206. Hordeum pratense.

1207. Hordeum murinum.

GRAMINEÆ. 295

1208. Hordeum maritimum.

1210. Agropyrum caninum.

1209. Agropyrum repens.

1211. Lolium perenne.

GRAMINEÆ.

1212. Lolium temulentum

1213. Brachypodium sylvaticum.

1214. Brachypodium pinnatum.

1215. Bromus erectus.

1216. Bromus asper

1217. Bromus sterilis.

1218. Bromus maximus.

1219. Bromus madritensis.

GRAMINEÆ.

1220. Bromus arvensis.

1222. Festuca ovina.

1221. Bromus giganteus.

1223. Festuca elatior.

GRAMINEÆ.

1224. Festuca sylvatica.

1226. Festuca uniglumis.

1225. Festuca Myuros.

1227. Dactylis glomerata.

GRAMINEÆ.

1228. Cynosurus cristatus.

1230 Briza media.

1229. Cynosurus echinatus.

1231. Briza minor.

GRAMINEÆ.

1232. Poa aquatica.

1233. Poa fluitans.

1234. Poa maritima.

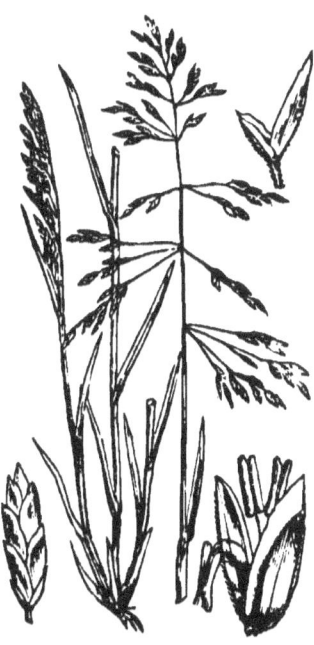
1235. Poa distans.

1236. Poa procumbens.

1237. Poa rigida.

1238. Poa loliacea.

1239. Poa annua.

GRAMINEÆ. 303

1240. Poa compressa.

1241. Poa pratensis.

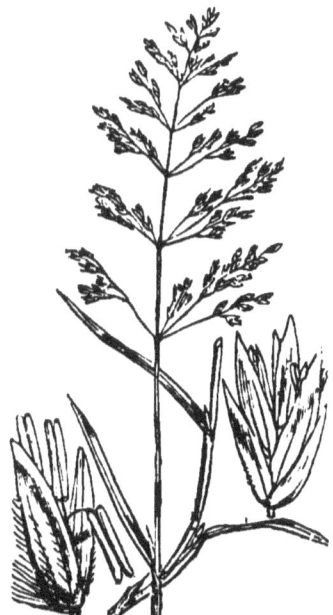
1242. Poa trivialis.

1243. Poa memoralis.

GRAMINEÆ.

1244. Poa laxa.

1245. Poa alpina.

1246. Poa bulbosa.

1247. Catabrosa aquatica.

GRAMINEÆ. 305

1248. Molinia cærulea.

1249. Melica nutans.

1250. Melica uniflora.

1251. Triodia decumbens.

x

GRAMINEÆ.

1252. Kœleria cristata.

1254. Arundo Phragmites.

1253. Sesleria cærulea.

1255. Lycopodium clavatum.

LYCOPODIACEÆ.

1256. Lycopodium annotinum.

1257. Lycopodium alpinum.

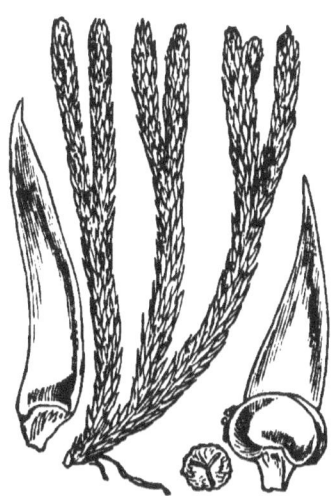

1258. Lycopodium Selago.

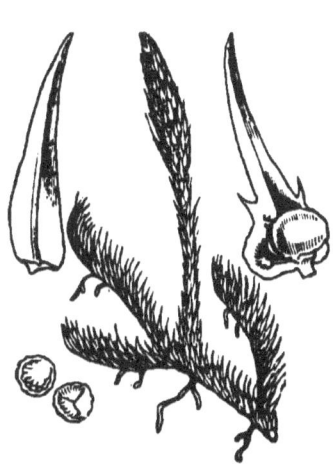

1259. Lycopodium inundatum.

SELAGINELLACEÆ.

1260. Selaginella selaginoides.

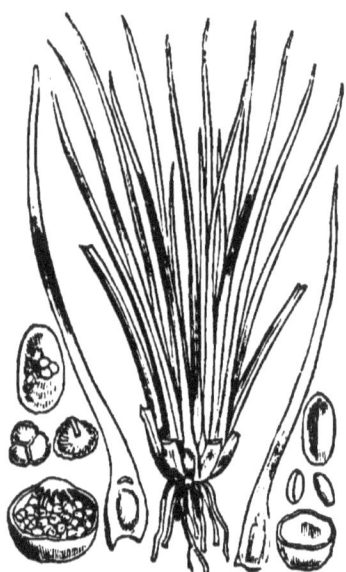

1261. Isoetes lacustris.

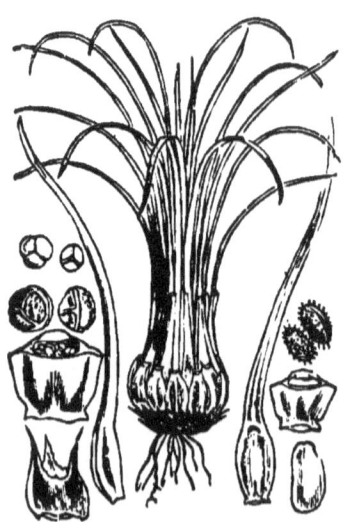

1261*. Isoetes Hystrix.

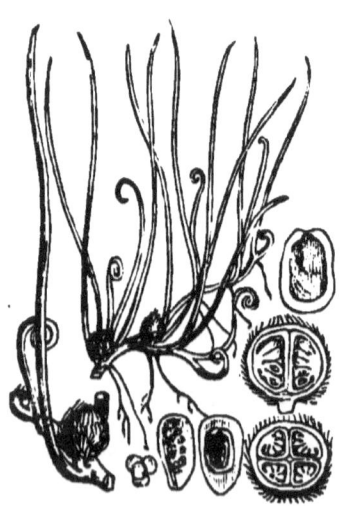

1262. Pilularia globulifera

EQUISETACEÆ.

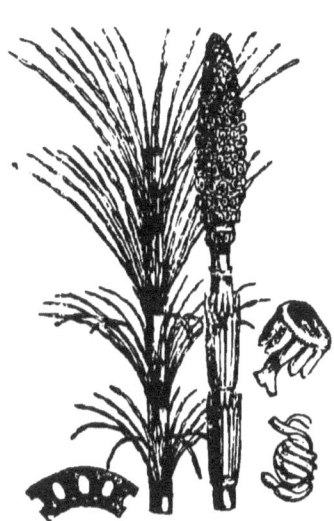

1263. Equisetum Telmateia.

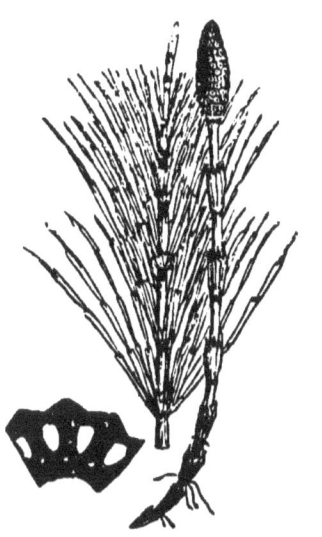

1264. Equisetum arvense.

1265. Equisetum sylvaticum.

1266. Equisetum pratense.

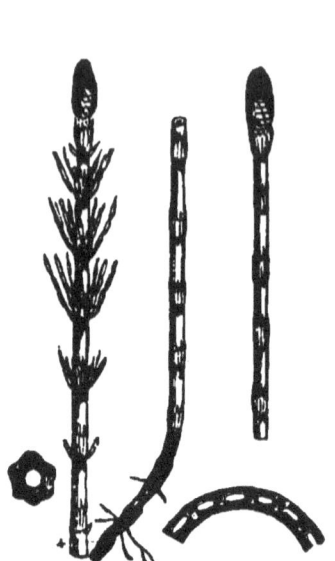
1267. Equisetum limosum.

1268. Equisetum littorale.

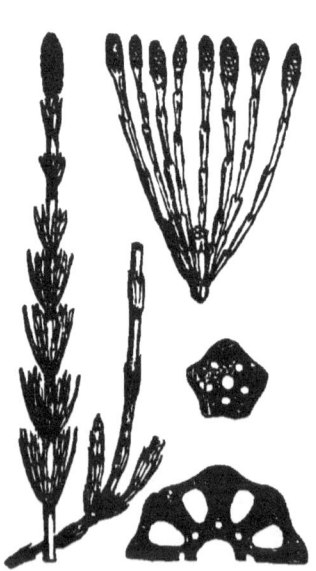
1269. Equisetum palustre.

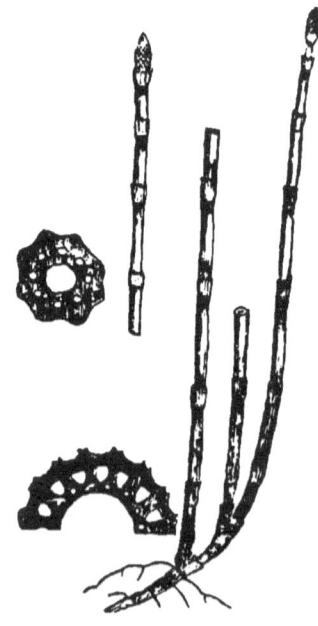
1270. Equisetum hyemale.

FILICES.

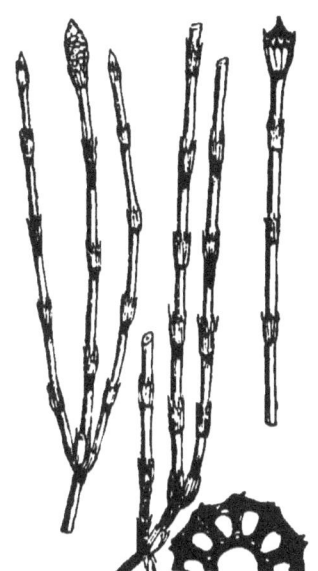

1271. Equisetum trachyodon.

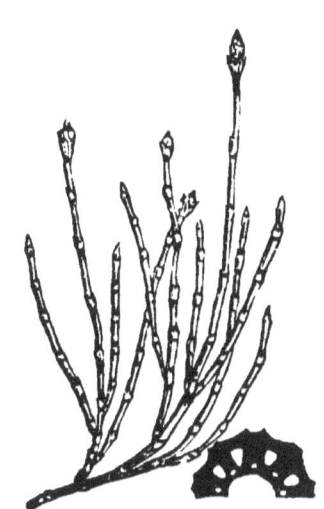

1272. Equisetum variegatum.

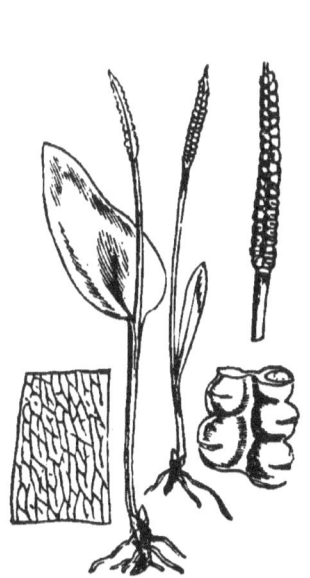

1273. Ophioglossum vulgatum.

1274. Botrychium Lunaria.

FILICES.

1275. Osmunda regalis.

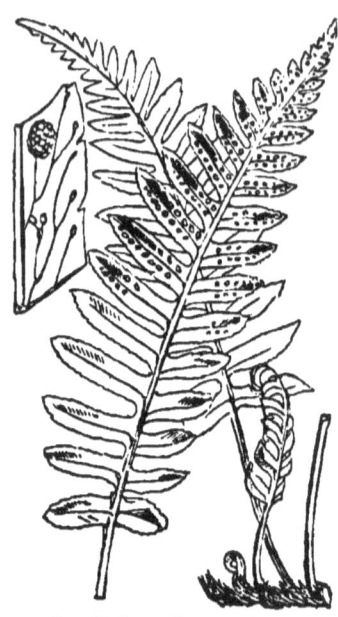

1276. Polypodium vulgare.

1277. Polypodium Phegopteris.

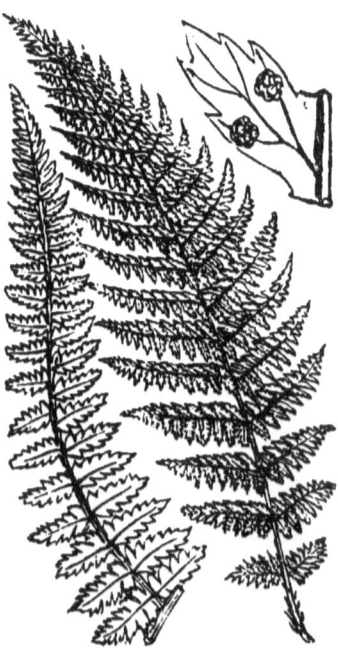

1278. Polypodium alpestre.

FILICES.

1279. Polypodium Dryopteris.

1280. Allosorus crispus.

1281. Grammitis leptophylla.

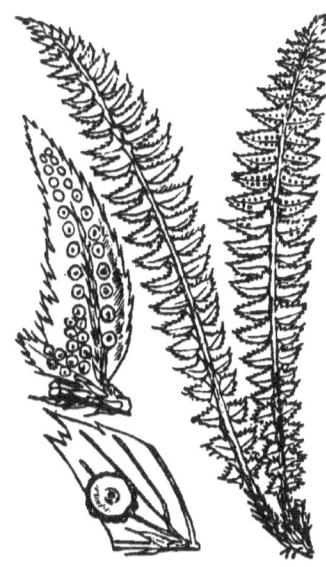

1282. Aspidium Lonchitis.

FILICES.

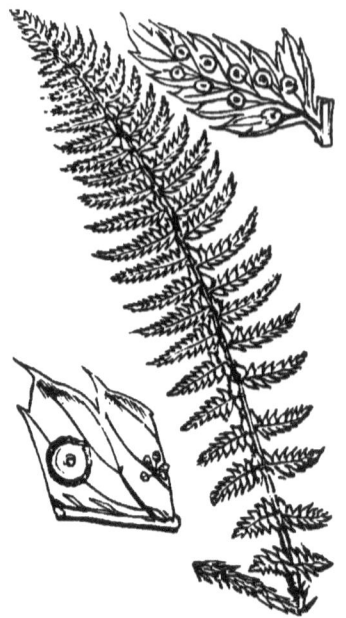

1283. Aspidium aculeatum.

1284. Aspidium Thelypteris.

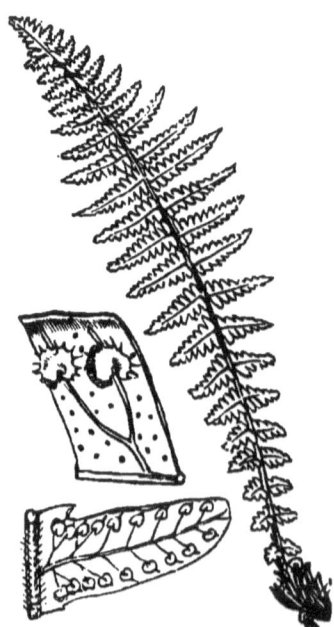

1285. Aspidium Oreopteris.

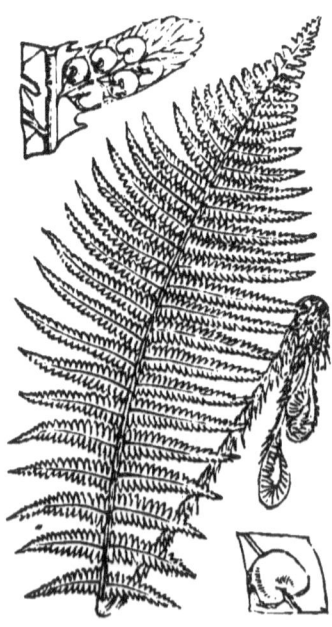

1286. Aspidium Filix-mas.

FILICES

1287. Aspidium cristatum.

1288. Aspidium spinulosum.

1289. Aspidium rigidum.

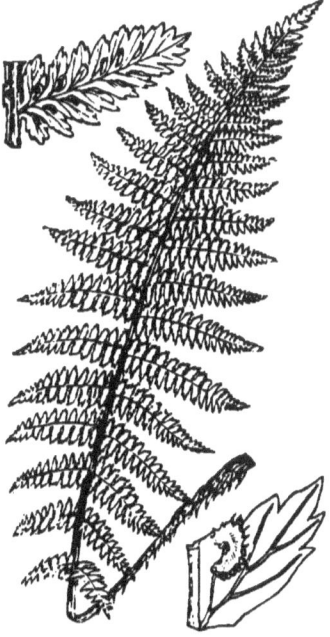

1290. Asplenium Filix-fœmina.

FILICES.

1291. Asplenium fontanum.

1292. Asplenium lanceolatum.

1293. Asplenium marinum.

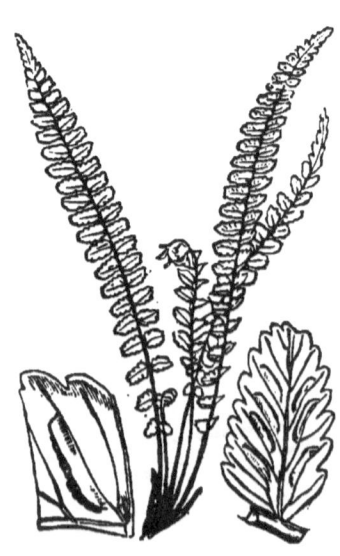

1294. Asplenium Trichomanes.

FILICES.

 1295. Asplenium viride.

 1296. Asplenium Adiantum-nigrum.

 1297. Asplenium Ruta-muraria.

 1298. Asplenium germanicum.

FILICES.

1299. Asplenium septentrionale.

1301. Ceterach officinarum.

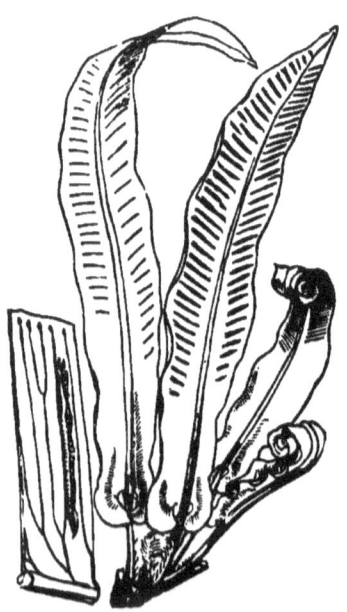

1300. Scolopendrium vulgare.

1302. Blechnum Spicant.

1303. Pteris aquilina.   1304. Adiantum Capillus-Veneris.

1305. Cystopteris fragilis.   1306. Cystopteris montana.

1307. Woodsia ilvensis.

1308. Trichomanes radicans.

1309. Hymenophyllum tunbridgense.

1310. Hymenophyllum unilaterale.

INDEX.

(Synonyms and names of varieties are in Italics.)

	FIG.		FIG.		FIG.
Acer campestre	220	Alchemilla alpina	823	*Anacamptis*	
Pseudo-platanus	221	*argentea*	323	*pyramidalis*	1003
Aceras anthropophora	1009	arvensis	324	*Anacharis Alsinastrum*	976
Achillea Millefolium	531	*conjuncta*	323	*canadensis*	976
Ptarmica	530	*hybrida*	322	Anagallis arvensis	653
Achyrophorus		*montana*	322	*cœrulea*	658
maculatus	585	vulgaris	322	*phœnicea*	658
Aconitum Napellus	30	Alisma *lanceolatum*	969	tenella	659
Acorus Calamus	943	natans	971	Anchusa *arvensis*	704
Actæa spicata	31	Plantago	969	officinalis	702
Actinocarpus		ranunculoides	970	sempervirens	703
Damasonium	972	*repens*	970	Andromeda polifolia	631
Adiantum		Alliaria officinalis	72	Anemone nemorosa	6
Capillus-Veneris	1304	Allium		Pulsatilla	5
Adonis autumnalis	7	Ampeloprasum	1046	Angelica sylvestris	432
Adoxa Moschatellina	459	*arenarium*	1047	Antennaria dioica	510
Ægopodium Podagraria	407	*Babingtonii*	1046	*hyperborea*	510
Æthusa cynapium	425	*carinatum*	1048	margaritacea	511
Agraphis nutans	1044	*compactum*	1051	Anthemis *anglica*	527
Agrimonia Eupatoria	327	*complanatum*	1048	arvensis	527
odorata	327	*Halleri*	1047	Cotula	526
Agropyrum *acutum*	1209	oleraceum	1048	*maritima*	527
caninum	1210	Porrum	1046	nobilis	528
littorale	1209	*rotundum*	1047	tinctoria	529
pycnanthemum	1209	Schœnoprasum	1049	Anthoxanthum	
repens	1209	scorodoprasum	1047	odoratum	1164
Agrostemma *githago*	142	*Sibiricum*	1049	*Puelii*	1164
Agrostis alba	1180	sphærocephalum	1050	*Anthriscus Cerefolium*	443
Anemagrostis	1183	triquetrum	1053	*sylvestris*	443
canina	1181	ursinum	1052	*vulgaris*	444
interrupta	1183	vineale	1051	Anthyllis *Dillenii*	267
nigra	1180	Allosorus crispus	1280	Vulneraria	267
pumila	1180	Alnus glutinosa	909	Antirrhinum majus	730
setacea	1182	Alopecurus agrestis	1172	Orontium	731
Spica-venti	1183	alpinus	1175	*Apargia autumnalis*	581
stolonifera	1180	*bulbosus*	1174	*hispida*	584
vulgaris	1180	*fulvus*	1174	*Taraxaci*	581
Aira *alpina*	1189	geniculatus	1174	Apera *interrupta*	1183
cæspitosa	1189	*palustris*	1174	*Spica-venti*	1183
canescens	1191	pratensis	1175	Apium graveolens	402
caryophyllea	1193	*pronus*	1174	inundatum	404
flexuosa	1190	Alsine *Cherleri*	149	nodiflorum	403
lævigata	1189	*stricta*	151	Aquilegia vulgaris	28
montana	1190	*tenuifolia*	152	Arabis ciliata	59
præcox	1192	*verna*	150	*glabrata*	58
setacea	1190	Althæa hirsuta	199	hirsuta	58
uliginosa	1190	officinalis	198	*hispida*	62
Ajuga Chamæpitys	819	Alyssum calycinum	86	perfoliata	56
genevensis	818	maritimum	87	petræa	62
pyramidalis	818	Ammophila		*sagittata*	58
reptans	817	arundinacea	1185	stricta	61

Y

	PIG.		PIG.		PIG.
Thaliana	60	remotum	1288	ruderalis	806
Turrita	57	rigidum	1289	Barbarea *arcuata*	51
Arbutus Unedo	628	spinulosum	1288	*intermedia*	51
Arctium *intermedium*	553	thelypteris	1284	*parviflora*	51
Lappa	553	Asplenium *acutum*	1296	*præcox*	51
majus	553	Adiantum-nigrum	1296	*stricta*	51
minus	553	*alternifolium*	1298	*vulgaris*	51
nemorosum	553	*anceps*	1294	Barkhausia *fœtida*	595
pubens	553	Ceterach	1301	*taraxacifolia*	594
tomentosum	553	*Clermontæ*	1294	Bartsia alpina	764
Arctostaphylos alpina	630	Filix-fœmina	1290	*divergens*	766
Uva-ursi	629	fontanum	1291	Odontites	766
Arenaria *Cherleri*	149	germanicum	1298	*serotina*	766
ciliata	155	*incisum*	1290	*verna*	766
Gerardi	150	lanceolatum	1292	viscosa	765
glutinosa	154	marinum	1293	Bellis perennis	502
hirta	150	*molle*	1290	Berberis vulgaris	83
hybrida	152	*obtusum*	1296	Beta maritima	850
laxa	152	*Petrarchæ*	1294	Betonica *officinalis*	798
leptoclados	154	*rhæticum*	1290	Betula alba	910
marginata	170	Ruta-muraria	1297	*glutinosa*	910
norwegica	155	septentrionale	1299	nana	901
peploides	153	*serpentini*	1296	*pendula*	910
rubella	150	Trichomanes	1294	*verrucosa*	910
rubra	170	viride	1295	Bidens cernua	519
serpyllifolia	154	Aster Linosyris	497	tripartita	520
sphærocarpa	154	Tripolium	496	Blechnum *boreale*	1302
tenuifolia	152	Astragalus alpinus	269	Spicant	1302
trinervis	156	*danicus*	268	Blysmus compressus	1087
uliginosa	151	glycyphyllos	270	rufus	1088
verna	150	hypoglottis	268	Borago officinalis	707
Armeria *duriuscula*	824	Astrantia major	398	Botrychium Lunaria	1274
maritima	824	*Athyrium Filix-*		*rutaceum*	1274
plantaginea	825	*fœmina*	1290	Brachypodium	
pubescens	824	Atriplex *angustifolia*	854	pinnatum	1214
pubigera	824	*arenaria*	855	sylvaticum	1213
vulgaris	824	*Babingtonia*	854	Brassica adpressa	83
Armoracia		*deltoidea*	854	alba	80
amphibium	55	*erecta*	854	*brevipes*	76
rusticana	84	*farinosa*	855	campestris	79
Arnoseris pusilla	608	*hastata*	854	*Cheiranthus*	77
Arrhenatherum		hortensis	853	monensis	77
avenaceum	1197	*laciniata*	855	muralis	76
elatius	1197	*litoralis*	854	*napus*	79
Artemisia Absinthium	537	*marina*	854	nigra	82
campestris	534	*nitens*	853	oleracea	78
gallica	535	patula	854	*polymorpha*	79
maritima	535	pedunculata	852	*Rapa*	79
vulgaris	536	portulacoides	851	*Ruta-baga*	79
Arum *italicum*	942	*prostrata*	854	Sinapis	81
maculatum	942	rosea	855	*Sinapistrum*	81
Arundo *Calamagrostis*	1187	*serrata*	854	tenuifolia	75
Phragmites	1254	*Smithii*	854	Briza media	1230
Asarum europæum	882	*triangularis*	854	minor	1231
Asparagus officinalis	1033	Atropa belladonna	715	Bromus arvensis	1220
Asperugo procumbens	708	Avena *alpina*	1195	asper	1216
Asperula *cynanchica*	480	*elatior*	1197	*Benekenii*	1216
odorata	479	fatua	1194	*commutatus*	1220
Aspidium aculeatum	1283	flavescens	1196	*diandrus*	1219
æmulum	1288	*planiculmis*	1195	erectus	1215
angulare	1283	pratensis	1195	giganteus	1221
Bootii	1288	pubescens	1195	*hordeaceus*	1220
cristatum	1267	*strigosa*	1194	madritensis	1219
dilatatum	1288	*Azalia procumbens*	632	maximus	1218
dumetorum	1288			*mollis*	1220
Filix-mas	1286			*multiflorus*	1220
lobatum	1283	Ballota *alba*	806	*pratensis*	1220
Lonchitis	1282	*fœtida*	806	*racemosus*	1220
Oreopteris	1285	nigra	806	*ramosus*	1216

INDEX.

	FIG.
rigidus	1219
seculinus	1220
serotinus	1216
sterilis	1217
velutinus	1220
Brunella vulgaris	793
Bryonia dioica	357
Bulbocastanum Linnæi	412
Bunium	
bulbocastanum	412
denudatum	441
flexuosum	441
Bupleurum aristatum	418
falcatum	420
Odontites	418
rotundifolium	417
tenuissimum	419
Butomus umbellatus	967
Buxus sempervirens	897
Cakile maritima	110
Calamagrostis	
Epigeios	1186
lanceolata	1187
lapponica	1188
stricta	1188
Calamintha Acinos	788
Clinopodium	790
menthæfolia	789
Nepeta	789
officinalis	789
sylvatica	789
Callitriche aquatica	900
autumnalis	900
hamulata	900
Lachii	900
obtusangula	900
pedunculata	900
platycarpa	900
stagnalis	900
truncata	900
verna	900
vernulis	900
Calluna vulgaris	640
Caltha palustris	24
radicans	24
Calystegia Sepium	685
Soldanella	686
Camelina fœtida	93
sativa	93
Campanula glomerata	615
hederacea	622
hybrida	623
latifolia	617
patula	620
persicifolia	620
Rapunculoides	618
rapunculus	619
rotundifolia	621
Trachelium	616
Capsella Bursa-pastoris	101
Cardamine amara	63
bulbifera	67
dentata	64
flexuosa	66
hastulata	62
hirsuta	66
impatiens	65
pratensis	64

	FIG.
sylvatica	66
Carduus acanthoides	558
acaulis	567
arvensis	562
crispus	558
eriophorus	563
Forsteri	566
heterophyllus	564
lanceolatus	560
Marianus	556
nutans	557
palustris	561
polyanthemus	558
pratensis	566
pycnocephalus	559
setosus	562
tenuiflorus	559
tuberosus	565
Woodwardsii	566
Carex acuta	1127
alpicola	1116
alpina	1128
ampullacea	1152
aquatilis	1126
arenaria	1122
argyroglochin	1112
atrata	1130
axillaris	1118
binervis	1142
Bœnninghauseniana	1118
Buxbaumii	1129
cæspitosa	1126
canescens	1116
capillaris	1145
ciliata	1132
clandestina	1131
collina	1134
curta	1116
Davalliana	1108
depauperata	1142
digitata	1132
dioica	1108
distans	1142
disticha	1122
divisa	1123
divulsa	1121
ebracteata	1138
echinata	1115
Ehrhartiana	1119
elongata	1114
erictetorum	1132
extensa	1140
filiformis	1137
flava	1141
frigida	1144
fulva	1142
Gibsoni	1126
glauca	1147
Goodenovii	1126
gracilis	1127
Grahami	1225
Grypos	1115
hirta	1138
hirtæformis	1138
Horuschuchiana	1142
humilis	1131
incurva	1124
intermedia	1122
involuta	1153

	FIG.
irrigua	1146
lævigata	1142
lagopina	1113
Leesii	1135
lepidocarpa	1141
leporina	1112
ligerica	1122
limosa	1146
Micheliana	1147
montana	1134
muricata	1121
Œderi	1141
ornithopoda	1132
ovalis	1112
pallescens	1139
paludosa	1154
panicea	1144
paniculata	1119
paradoxa	1119
pauciflora	1111
pendula	1151
Persoonii	1116
phæostachya	1144
pilulifera	1135
polygama	1129
præcox	1133
Pseudocyperus	1150
Pseudo-divulsa	1121
Pseudo-paradoxa	1119
pulicaris	1109
pulla	1125
punctata	1143
rariflora	1146
recurva	1147
remota	1117
rigida	1126
riparia	1154
rupestris	1110
salina	1144
saxatilis	1125
Saxumbra	1135
scotica	1144
spadicea	1154
sparsiflora	1144
speirostachya	1142
spicata	1121
stellulata	1115
stictocarpa	1147
stricta	1126
strigosa	1149
sylvatica	1148
tenella	1117
teretiuscula	1119
tomentosa	1136
tricostata	1127
trinervis	1126
vaginata	1144
Vahlii	1127
vesicaria	1153
vitilis	1116
vulgaris	1126
vulpina	1120
Watsoni	1126
Xanthocarpa	1142
Carlina vulgaris	569
Carpinus Betulus	912
Carum Bulbocastanum	412
Carvi	411
flexuosum	441

	FIG.
Petroselinum	408
segetum	409
verticillatum	410
Catabrosa aquatica	1247
Caucalis Anthriscus	446
arvensis	447
daucoides	448
helvetica	447
infesta	447
latifolia	449
nodosa	445
Centaurea aspera	573
Calcitrapa	574
Cyanus	572
decipiens	570
Isnardi	573
nigra	570
nigrescens	570
Scabiosa	571
solstitialis	575
Centranthus ruber	482
Centunculus minimus	660
Cephalanthera ensifolia	985
grandiflora	984
pallens	984
rubra	986
Cerastium alpinum	161
aquaticum	163
arvense	160
atrovirens	159
glomeratum	159
glutinosum	159
holosteoides	159
lanatum	161
latifolium	161
pumilum	159
quaternellum	157
semidecandrum	159
tetrandrum	159
trigynum	162
triviale	159
viscosum	159
vulgatum	159
Ceratophyllum	
apiculatum	899
demersum	899
submersum	899
Ceterach officinarum	1301
Chærophyllum	
Anthriscus	444
sativum	443
sylvestre	443
temulentum	442
temulum	442
Chamagrostis minima	1174
Cheiranthus cheiri	50
Chelidonium	
laciniatum	42
majus	42
Chenopodina maritima	839
Chenopodium	
acutifolium	842
album	843
Bonus-henricus	849
botryoides	845
candicans	843
deltoideum	846
ficifolium	843
glaucum	814

	FIG.
hybridum	848
intermedium	846
murale	847
olidum	841
paganum	843
polyspermum	842
rubrum	845
urbicum	846
viride	843
Vulvaria	841
Cherleria sedoides	140
Chlora perfoliata	680
Chrysanthemum	
inodorum	524
Leucanthemum	521
Parthenium	523
segetum	522
Chrysocoma Linosyris	497
Chrysosplenium	
alternifolium	388
oppositifolium	387
Cicendia filiformis	672
pusilla	673
Cichorium Intybus	607
Cicuta virosa	401
Cineraria integrifolia	550
Circæa alpina	353
intermedia	353
lutetiana	352
Cirsium anglicum	566
Cistus anglicus	117
marifolius	117
tomentosus	118
Cladium germanicum	1094
Mariscus	1094
Claytonia alsinoides	173
perfoliata	173
Clematis Vitalba	1
Clinopodium vulgare	790
Cnicus acaulis	567
arvensis	562
Carolorum	564
dubius	567
eriophorus	563
Forsteri	566
heterophyllus	564
lanceolatus	560
palustris	561
pratensis	566
setosus	562
tuberosus	565
Woodwardi	566
Cochlearea alpina	85
anglica	85
Armoracia	84
danica	85
grœnlandica	85
littoralis	85
officinalis	85
polymorpha	85
Colchicum autumnale	1057
Comarum palustre	320
Conium maculatum	451
Conopodium	
denudatum	441
Convallaria majalis	1031
Convolvulus arvensis	684
sepium	685
Soldanella	686

	FIG.
Conyza squarrosa	515
Corallorhiza innata	981
Coriandrum sativum	454
Cornus sanguinea	458
suecica	457
Coronopus didyma	108
Ruellii	107
Corrigiola littoralis	832
Corydalis bulbosa	47
claviculata	47
lutea	46
solida	47
Corylus Avellana	913
Corynephorus	
canescens	1191
Cotoneaster vulgaris	339
Cotyledon Umbilicus	359
Crambe maritima	111
Cratægus monogyna	338
Oxyacantha	338
Oxyacanthoides	338
Crepis biennis	597
fœtida	595
hieracioides	598
paludosa	599
setosa	594
succisæfolia	598
taraxacifolia	594
tectorum	598
virens	596
Crithmum maritimum	431
Crocus nudiflorus	1021
speciosus	1021
vernus	1020
Cryptogramme crispa	1280
Cucubalus Behen	134
Cuscuta Epilinum	688
Epithymum	689
europæa	687
Trifolii	689
Cyclamen europæum	651
hederæfolium	651
neapolitanum	651
Cynodon Dactylon	1200
Cynoglossum	
montanum	710
officinale	709
sylvaticum	710
Cynosurus cristatus	1228
echinatus	1229
Cyperus fuscus	1082
longus	1081
Cypripedium	
Calceolus	1014
Cystopteris alpina	1305
dentata	1305
Dickieana	1305
fragilis	1305
montana	1306
Cytisus scoparius	231
Dabeocia polifolia	633
Dactylis glomerata	1227
Damasonium stellatum	972
Danthonia decumbens	1251
Daphne Laureola	879
Mezereum	878
Datura Stramonium	711

INDEX. 325

	FIG.
Daucus Carota	450
gummifer	450
maritimus	450
Delphinium Ajacis	29
Consolida	29
Demazeria loliacea	1223
Dentaria bulbifera	67
Deschampsia cæspitosa	1189
flexuosa	1190
Deyeuxia neglecta	1188
Dianthus Armeria	129
cæsius	131
Caryophyllus	131
deltoides	130
glaucus	130
plumarius	131
prolifer	128
Digitalis purpurea	747
Digitaria filiformis	1158
humifusa	1158
sanguinalis	1157
Digraphis arundinacea	1166
Diotis maritima	532
Diplotaxis muralis	76
tenuifolia	75
Dipsacus Fullonum	490
pilosus	491
sylvestris	490
Doronicum	
Pardalianches	551
plantagineum	552
Draba aizoides	88
confusa	90
contorta	90
hirta	89
incana	90
muralis	91
rupestris	89
verna	92
Drosera anglica	392
intermedia	391
longifolia	391
rotundifolia	390
Dryas depressa	303
octopetala	303
Echinochloa Crus-galli	1162
Echium italicum	690
Plantagineum	691
violaceum	691
vulgare	690
Elatine hexandra	176
Hydropiper	177
tripetala	176
Eleocharis acicularis	1089
cæspitosa	1094
multicaulis	1092
palustris	1091
parvula	1090
pauciflora	1093
uniglumis	1041
Watsoni	1041
Elcogiton fluitans	1095
Elisma natans	871
Elodea canadensis	976
Elymus arenarius	1204
europæus	1205
geniculatus	1204

	FIG.
Empetrum nigrum	898
Endymion nutans	1044
Enodium cœruleum	1248
Epilobium alpinum	349
alsinefolium	348
anagallidifolium	349
angustifolium	341
brachycarpum	341
hirsutum	342
intermedium	343
lanceolatum	344
montanum	344
obscurum	346
palustre	347
parviflorum	343
rivulare	343
roseum	345
tetragonum	346
virgatum	346
Epipactis atro-rubens	982
Helleborine	982
latifolia	982
media	982
ovalis	982
palustris	983
purpurata	982
rubiginosa	982
violacea	982
viridiflora	982
Epipogium aphyllum	990
Gmelini	990
Equisetum arenarium	1272
arvense	1264
Drummondii	1266
fluviatile	1263
hyemale	1270
limosum	1267
littorale	1268
Mackaii	1271
maximum	1263
Mourei	1270
pulceaceum	1270
palustre	1269
pratense	1266
ramosum	1271
sylvaticum	1265
Telmateia	1263
trachyodon	1271
umbrosum	1266
variegatum	1272
Wilsoni	1272
Erica carnea	638
ciliaris	637
cinerea	635
hibernica	638
Mackaiana	636
Mackayi	636
mediterranea	638
Tetralix	636
vagans	639
vulgaris	640
Erigeron acris	498
alpinus	499
canadensis	500
uniflorus	499
Eriocaulon	
septangulare	1080
Eriophorum alpinum	1104
angustifolium	1106

	FIG.
gracile	1106
latifolium	1106
polystachyum	1106
pubescens	1106
vaginatum	1105
Erodium chærophyllum	213
cicutarium	213
comniætum	213
hirtum	213
maritimum	215
moschatum	214
pimpinellæfolium	213
Erophila brachycarpa	92
inflata	92
vulgaris	92
Erucastrum incana	83
Eryngium campestre	400
maritimum	399
obovata	392
Erysimum Alliaria	72
cheiranthoides	73
orientale	74
Erythræa capitata	674
Centaurium	674
chloodes	674
conferta	674
latifolia	674
linarifolia	674
littoralis	674
pulchella	674
Eupatorium	
cannabinum	495
Euphorbia	
amygdaloides	894
Cyparissias	893
Esula	893
exigua	889
Helioscopia	884
hiberna	886
Lathyris	890
palustris	887
Paralias	892
Peplis	883
Peplus	888
pilosa	887
platyphyllos	885
portlandica	891
segetalis	891
stricta	885
Euphrasia gracilis	767
nemorosa	767
Odontites	766
officinalis	767
rotundata	766
viscosa	765
Evonymus europæus	223
Fagus sylvatica	914
Falcatula	
ornithopodioides	243
Fedia Auricula	488
carinata	487
dentata	489
olitoria	486
Festuca ambigua	1225
arenaria	1222
arundinacea	1223
bromoides	1225

INDEX.

	FIG.
cæsia	1222
Calamaria	1224
decidua	1224
duriuscula	1222
elatior	1223
gigantea	1221
glauca	1222
loliacea	1223
Myurus	1225
oraria	1222
ovina	1222
pratensis	1223
Pseudo-myurus	1225
rigida	1237
rubra	1222
sciuroides	1225
subulicola	1222
sylvatica	1224
tenuifolia	1222
triflora	1221
uniglumis	1226
vivipara	1222
Filago apiculata	503
canescens	503
gallica	505
germanica	503
Jussiæi	503
lutescens	503
minima	504
montana	504
spathulata	503
Fœniculum officinale	426
vulgare	426
Fragaria elatior	311
sterilis	312
vesca	311
Frankenia lævis	127
Fraxinus excelsior	668
heterophylla	668
Fritillaria Meleagris	1035
Fumaria agraria	45
Boræi	45
capreolata	45
confusa	45
densiflora	45
media	45
micrantha	45
muralis	45
officinalis	45
pallidiflora	45
parviflora	45
tenuisecta	45
Vaillantii	45
Gagea lutea	1038
Galanthus nivalis	1024
Galeobdolon luteum	812
Galeopsis dubia	804
Ladanum	803
ochroleuca	804
speciosa	805
Tetrahit	805
versicolor	805
Galium anglicum	475
Aparine	477
aristatum	474
boreale	476

	FIG.
commutatum	473
Cruciata	469
erectum	474
Mollugo	474
montanum	473
palustre	471
parisiense	475
pusillum	473
saxatile	473
spurium	477
sylvestre	473
tricorne	478
uliginosum	472
Vaillantii	477
verum	470
Gastridium	
lendigerum	1184
Genista anglica	230
humifusa	228
pilosa	229
tinctoria	228
Gentiana Amarella	678
campestris	679
germanica	678
nivalis	677
Pneumonanthe	675
uliginosa	678
verna	676
Geranium	
carolinianum	211
columbinum	212
dissectum	211
lancastriense	201
lucidum	207
molle	208
perenne	205
phæum	202
pratense	204
purpureum	206
pusillum	209
pyrenaicum	205
Robertianum	206
rotundifolium	210
sanguineum	201
sylvaticum	203
Geum intermedium	305
rivale	305
urbanum	304
Githago segetum	142
Gladiolus communis	1017
illyricus	1017
Glaucium luteum	44
violaceum	43
Glaux maritima	657
Glechoma hederacea	791
Glyce maritima	87
Glyceria aquatica	1232
Borreri	1235
conferta	1235
declinata	1233
distans	1235
fluitans	1233
loliacea	1238
maritima	1234
pedicellata	1233
plicata	1233
procumbens	1236
rigida	1237
spectabilis	1232

	FIG.
Gnaphalium	
luteo-album	506
norvegicum	507
pilulare	509
rectum	507
supinum	508
sylvaticum	507
uliginosum	509
Goodyera repens	994
Gramnitis leptophylla	1281
Gymnadenia albida	1007
conopsea	1005
Gymnogramma lepto-	
phylla	1281
Habenaria albida	1007
bifolia	1004
chlorantha	1004
conopsea	1005
intacta	1006
viridis	1008
Haloscias scoticum	428
Hedera canariensis	455
Helix	455
Hedypnois hirtus	582
hispidus	580
Taraxaci	581
Helianthemum	
Breweri	116
canum	117
guttatum	116
polifolium	119
surrejanum	118
vineale	117
vulgare	118
Heliocharis, see Eleocharis.	
Helleborus fœtidus	27
viridis	26
Helminthia echioides	578
Helosciadium	
inundatum	404
repens	403
Heracleum	
angustifolium	437
Sphondylium	437
Herminium Monorchis	1010
Herniaria ciliata	833
glabra	833
hirsuta	833
Hesperis matronalis	68
Hieracium acutifolium	608
aggregatum	602
alpinum	601
anglicum	603
argenteum	602
atratum	601
auraniiacum	600
boreale	605
Borreri	606
cæsium	602
calenduliflorum	601
canadense	604
cerinthoides	603
chrysanthum	601
cinerascens	602
corymbosum	606
crocatum	606
decipiens	603
denticulatum	606

INDEX. 327

	FIG.
Dewari	602
divaricatum	601
eximium	601
filifolium	604
flocculosum	602
Gibsoni	602
globosum	601
gothicum	602
gracilentum	601
heterophyllum	605
holosericeum	601
hypochœroides	602
inuloides	606
Iricum	603
juranum	606
Lapyrousii	603
lasiophyllum	602
Lawsoni	601
lingulatum	601
maculatum	602
melanocephalum	601
molle	598
murorum	602
nigrescens	601
nitidum	602
obtusifolium	602
pallidum	602
paludosum	599
Peleterianum	600
Pilosella	600
pilosissimum	600
prenanthoides	606
pulmonarium	601
rigidum	606
sabaudum	605
saxifragum	601
senescens	601
stelligerum	602
strictum	606
sylvaticum	602
tenellum	601
tridentatum	602
umbellatum	604
villosum	601
vulgatum	602
Hierochloe borealis	1163
Hippocrepis comosa	275
Hippophae rhamnoides	880
Hippuris vulgaris	395
Holcus lanatus	1198
mollis	1199
Holosteum umbellatum	158
Honckenya peploides	153
Hordeum maritimum	1208
murinum	1207
pratense	1206
sylvaticum	1205
Hottonia palustris	647
Humulus Lupulus	905
Hutchinsia petræa	100
Hyacinthus nonscriptus	1044
Hydrocharis Morsus-ranæ	977
Hydrocotyle vulgaris	396
Hymenophyllum alatum	1308
tunbridgense	1309
unilaterale	1310

	FIG.
Wilsoni	1310
Hyoscyamus niger	712
pallidus	712
Hypericum Audrosæmum	179
anglicum	179
bœticum	182
calycinum	178
decumbens	184
dubium	181
Elodes	188
hirsutum	186
humifusum	183
linariifolium	184
montanum	187
perforatum	180
pulchrum	185
quadrangulum	182
tetrapterum	182
undulatum	182
Hypochœris Balbisii	583
glabra	583
maculata	585
radicata	584
Hypopethys multiflora	646
Iberis amara	99
Ilex Aquifolium	222
Illecebrum verticillatum	834
Impatiens fulva	219
Noli-me-tangere	218
parviflora	218
Inula Conyza	515
crithmoides	514
dysenterica	516
Helenium	512
Pulicaria	517
salicina	513
Iris acoriformis	1015
fœtidissima	1014
Pseudacorus	1015
Isatis tinctoria	109
Isnardia palustris	351
Isoetes Duriæi	1261
echinospora	1260
hystrix	1261
lacustris	1261
Morei	1260
Isolepis fluitans	1095
Holoschœnus	1098
pygmæa	1097
Savinna	1097
Savii	1097
setacea	1096
Jasione montana	612
Juncus acutiflorus	1062
acutus	1071
arcticus	1061
articulatus	1062
balticus	1061
biglumis	1074
bottnicus	1064
bufonius	1067
bulbosus	1064
capitatus	1069
castaneus	1073

	FIG.
cœnosus	1064
communis	1058
compressus	1064
conglomeratus	1058
diffusus	1059
effusus	1058
filiformis	1060
Gerardi	1064
glaucus	1059
glomeratus	1058
lamprocarpus	1062
maritimus	1070
nigritellus	1062
obtusiflorus	1063
pygmæus	1068
squarrosus	1066
subverticillatus	1062
supinus	1062
sylvaticus	1062
tenuis	1065
trifidus	1072
triglumis	1074
uliginosus	1062
Juniperus communis	935
nana	935
Knappia agrostidea	1176
Knautia arvensis	494
Kobresia caricina	1107
Kœleria cristata	1252
Koniga maritima	87
Lactuca alpina	589
muralis	586
saligna	588
Scariola	587
virosa	587
Lagurus ovatus	1177
Lamium album	810
amplexicaule	808
dissectum	809
Galeobdolon	812
hybridum	809
incisum	809
intermedium	808
maculatum	811
purpureum	809
Lapsana communis	609
pusilla	608
Lastrea abbreviata	1286
æmula	1289
collina	1288
cristata	1287
dilatata	1288
Filix-mas	1286
Oreopteris	1285
recurva	1289
rigida	1289
spinulosa	1288
Thelypteris	1284
uliginosa	1287
Lathræa squamaria	723
Lathyrus Aphaca	288
hirsutus	289
latifolius	292
macrorrhizus	295
maritimus	294

INDEX

	FIG.
niger	296
Nissolia	287
palustris	293
pratensis	290
sylvestris	292
tuberosus	291
Lavatera arborea	194
Olbia	194
Leersia oryzoides	1155
Lemna arrhiza	948
gibba	946
Michelii	948
minor	945
polyrrhiza	947
trisulca	944
Leontodon autumnalis	581
hastilis	580
hirtus	582
hispidus	580
pratensis	581
Taraxacum	593
Leonurus Cardiaca	807
Lepidium campestre	102
Draba	104
hirtum	102
latifolium	105
ruderale	106
Smithii	103
Lepigonum medium	170
neglectum	170
rubrum	170
rupestre	170
rupicola	170
salinum	170
Lepturus filiformis	1202
incurvatus	1202
Leucoium æstivum	1025
vernum	1025
Libanotis montana	427
Ligusticum scoticum	428
Ligustrum vulgare	669
Limnanthemum nymphæoides	682
peltatum	682
Limosella aquatica	744
Linaria Cymbalaria	737
Elatine	739
latifolia	732
minor	736
Pelisseriana	734
repens	733
sepium	733
speciosa	732
spuria	738
striata	733
supina	735
vulgaris	732
Linnæa borealis	467
Linosyris vulgaris	497
Linum angustifolium	191
catharticum	192
perenne	190
usitatissimum	189
Liparis Loeselii	980
Listera cordata	988
ovata	987
Litho-spermum arvense	694
officinale	695
purpureo-cæruleum	696

	FIG.
Littorella lacustris	831
Lloydia serotina	1037
Lobelia Dortmanna	610
urens	611
Lobularia maritima	87
Loiseleuria procumbens	632
Lolium arvense	1212
italicum	1211
multiflorum	1211
perenne	1211
remotum	1211
temulentum	1212
Lomaria Spicant	1302
Lonicera Caprifolium	465
Periclymenum	464
Xylosteum	466
Lotus angustissimus	266
corniculatus	265
crassifolius	265
decumbens	265
deflexus	266
diffusus	266
hirsutus	265
hispidus	265
major	265
tenuifolius	265
tenuis	265
uliginosus	265
Ludwigia palustris	351
Luzula arcuata	1077
Borreri	1075
campestris	1078
congesta	1078
erecta	1078
Forsteri	1075
maxima	1076
multiflora	1078
pilosa	1075
spicata	1079
sylvatica	1076
vernalis	1075
Lychnis alba	140
alpina	145
dioica	141
dirurna	141
Flos-cuculi	143
Githago	142
vespertina	140
Viscaria	144
Lycopodium alpinum	1257
annotinum	1256
clavatum	1255
comp.anatum	1257
inundatum	1259
selaginoides	1260
Selago	1258
Lycopsis arvensis	704
Lycopus europæus	777
Lynosiris vulgaris	497
Lysimachia nemorum	655
Nummularia	654
punctata	652
thyrsiflora	653
vulgaris	652
Lythrum hyssopifolium	355
Salicaria	354
Maianthemum bifolium	1032

	FIG.
Convalaria	1032
Malachium aquaticum	163
Malaxis paludosa	979
Malva moschata	197
parviflora	195
pusila	195
rotundifolia	195
sylvestris	196
verticillata	195
Marrubium vulgare	797
Matricaria Chamomilla	525
inodora	524
maritima	524
Parthenium	523
Matthiola incana	48
sinuata	49
Meconopsis cambrica	41
Medicago apiculata	237
denticulata	237
falcata	234
lappacea	237
lupulina	236
maculata	238
minima	239
sativa	235
sylvestris	234
Melachium aquaticum	163
Melampyrum arvense	772
cristatum	771
montanum	773
pratense	773
sylvaticum	774
Melica nutans	1249
uniflora	1250
Melilotus alba	242
altissima	240
arvensis	241
leucantha	242
officinalis	240
vulgaris	242
Melittis grandiflora	796
Melissophyllum	796
Mentha agrestis	784
Allioni	784
alopecuroides	778
aquatica	782
arvensis	784
cardiaca	783
citrata	782
gentilis	783
gracilis	783
hircina	782
hirsuta	782
mollissima	778
nemorosa	778
nummularia	784
officinalis	781
paludosa	783
palustris	782
parietariæfolia	784
Pauliana	783
piperita	781
præcox	784
pratensis	783
pubescens	782
Pulegium	785
rotundifolia	779
rubra	783
sativa	783

	FIG.		FIG.		FIG.
subglabra	782	*terrestre*	54	pyramidalis	1003
sylvestris	778	*Neotinia intacta*	1006	*Simia*	996
velutina	783	Neottia Nidus-avis	989	*tephrosanthos*	996
viridis	780	Nepeta Cataria	792	ustulata	997
vulgaris	781	Glechoma	791	Origanum	
Wirtgeniana	783	*Nephrodium æmulum*	1288	*megastachyum*	787
Menyanthes trifoliata	681	*cristatum*	1287	vulgare	787
Menziesia cærulea	634	*dilatatum*	1288	Ornithogalum nutans	1040
polifolia	633	*Filix-mas*	1286	pyrenaicum	1041
Mercurialis *ambigua*	896	*fœnisecii*	1288	umbellatum	1039
annua	896	montanum	1285	Ornithopus ebracteatus	273
perennis	895	*Oreopteris*	1285	perpusillus	274
Mertensia maritima	193	remotum	1288	Orobanche *amethystea*	720
Mespilus germanica	340	*rigidum*	1289	*arenaria*	721
Meum athamanticum	430	*spinulosum*	1288	*barbata*	720
Mibora verna	1176	*Thelypteris*	1284	cærulea	721
Microcala filiformis	672	Nuphar *intermedium*	35	caryophyllacea	717
Milium effusum	1156	luteum	35	elatior	719
Mimulus luteus	744	*pumilum*	35	*Epithymum*	718
Mœhringia trinervia	156	Nymphæa alba	34	*Eryngii*	720
Mœnchia erecta	157			*Galii*	717
Molinia cærulea	1248	*Odontites divergens*	766	*Hederæ*	720
depauperata	1248	*rotundata*	766	major	716
Moneses grandiflora	641	*rubra*	766	minor	720
Monotropa Hypopitys	646	*serotina*	766	*Picridis*	720
Montia fontana	174	*verna*	766	ramosa	722
minor	174	Œnanthe crocata	423	*Rapum*	716
rivularis	174	fistulosa	421	rubra	718
Mulgedium alpinum	589	*fluviatilis*	424	Orobus macrorrhizus	295
Muscari racemosum	1045	*Lachenalii*	422	*niger*	296
Myosotis *alpestris*	698	*peucedanifolia*	422	*sylvaticus*	281
arvensis	699	Phellandrium	424	*tenuifolius*	295
cæspitosa	697	pimpinelloides	422	*tuberosus*	295
collina	700	*silaifolia*	422	Osmunda regalis	1275
lingulata	697	*Smithii*	422	Oxalis Acetosella	216
Mitteni	700	Œnothera biennis	350	corniculata	217
palustris	697	*odorata*	350	*stricta*	217
repens	697	Onobrychis sativa	276	*Oxycoccus palustris*	627
rupicola	698	Ononis *antiquorum*	236	Oxyria *digyna*	866
strigulosa	697	arvensis	232	reniformis	866
sylvatica	698	*campestris*	232	Oxytropis campestris	271
versicolor	701	*inermis*	232	*Halleri*	272
Myosurus minimus	8	*procumbens*	232	uralensis	272
Myrica Gale	908	*procurrens*	232		
Myriophyllum		reclinata	233	Pæonia officinalis	32
alterniflorum	393	*repens*	232	*corallina*	32
pectinatum	394	*spinosa*	232	Panicum Crus-galli	1162
spicatum	393	Onopordon Acanthium	568	glabrum	1158
verticillatum	394	Ophioglossum		glaucum	1160
Myrrhis odorota	410	*lusitanicum*	1273	sanguinale	1157
		vulgatum	1273	verticillatum	1159
Naias flexilis	951	Ophrys apifera	1011	viride	1161
graminea	953	*arachnites*	1011	Papaver Argemone	40
major	952	aranifera	1012	dubium	38
marina	952	*fucifera*	1012	hybridum	39
Narcissus biflorus	1023	muscifera	1013	*Lamottei*	38
Bromfeldii	1022	*Trollii*	1011	*Lecoqii*	38
combricus	1022	Orchis *fusca*	996	Rhœas	37
lobularis	1022	hircina	1002	somniferum	36
major	1022	*incarnata*	1001	Parietaria *diffusa*	904
Pseudonarcissus	1022	latifolia	1001	officinalis	904
Nardus stricta	1203	laxiflora	999	Paris quadrifolia	1027
Narthecium		maculata	1000	Parnassia palustris	389
ossifragum	1055	*majalis*	1001	Pastinaca sativa	436
Nasturtium amphibium	55	mascula	998	Pedicularis palustris	769
officinale	52	militaris	996	sylvatica	770
palustre	54	Morio	995	Peplis Portula	356
siifolium	52	*palmata*	1001	*Petasites vulgaris*	539
sylvestre	53	*purpurea*	996	*Petroselinum sativum*	408

330   INDEX.

	FIG.		FIG.		FIG.
Peucedanum officinale	433	procumbens . .	1236	*filiformis* . . .	966
Ostruithium .	435	rigida . . .	1237	*flabelatus* . . .	966
palustre . . .	434	*stricta* . . .	1244	*fluitans* . . .	956
sativum . . .	436	*strigosa* . . .	1241	*Friesii* . . .	965
Phaca astragalina .	269	*sub-cærulea* . .	1241	*gracilis* . . .	965
Phalaris *arundinacea* .	1166	*sub-compressa* . .	1240	*gramineus* . .	963
canariensis . .	1165	trivialis . . .	1242	*Griffithii* . . .	959
Phellandrium		Polemonium cæruleum	683	heterophyllus . .	957
aquaticum . .	424	Polycarpon		*juncifolius* . .	966
Phleum alpinum .	1168	tetraphyllum . .	172	*lanceolatus* . .	958
arenarium . .	1171	Polygala *amara* . .	126	*lithuanicus* . .	959
asperum . . .	1170	*austriaca* . .	126	*Lonchites* . .	958
Bœhmeri . .	1169	*calcarea* . . .	126	*longifolius* . .	958
nodosum . . .	1167	*ciliata* . . .	126	lucens . . .	958
phalaroides . .	1169	*depressa* . . .	126	*marinus* . . .	966
pratense . . .	1167	*oxyptera* . . .	126	*mucronatus* . .	965
Phragmites communis.	1254	*serpyllana* . .	126	natans . . .	956
Phyllodoce cærulea .	634	*uliginosa* . . .	126	*nitens* . . .	957
taxifolia . . .	634	vulgaris . . .	126	*oblongus* . . .	956
Physospermum		Polygonatum		obtusifolius . .	963
cornubiense . .	452	multiflorum . .	1029	pectinatus . .	966
Phyteuma orbiculare .	613	officinale . . .	1030	perfoliatus . .	960
spicatum . . .	614	verticillatum . .	1028	*plantagineus* . .	956
Picris *arvalis* . .	579	Polygonum amphibium	873	*polygonifolius* . .	956
echioides . .	578	aviculare . . .	867	præelongus . .	959
hieracioides . .	579	*biforme* . . .	874	pusillus . . .	965
Pilularia globulifera .	1262	Bistorta . . .	872	*rufescens* . . .	958
Pimpinella *dioica* .	406	Convolvulus . .	869	*salicifolius* . .	959
glauca . . .	406	dumetorum . .	870	*serratus* . . .	961
magna . . .	416	*flexile* . . .	1278	*spathulatus* . .	958
major . . .	416	Hydropiper . .	876	*trichoides* . .	963
Saxifraga . .	415	lapathifolium . .	875	*Zizii* . . .	958
Pinguicula alpina .	663	*laxum* . . .	875	*Zosterifolius* . .	964
grandiflora . .	662	*littorale* . . .	867	Potentila *alpestris* .	316
lusitanica . .	664	*maculatum* . .	875	anserina . .	318
vulgaris . . .	662	maritimum . .	868	argentea . . .	315
Pinus sylvestris . .	934	minus . . .	877	aurea . . .	316
Pisum maritimum .	294	*mite* . . .	877	Comarum . .	320
Plantago Coronopus .	830	*nodosum* . . .	875	Fragariastrum . .	312
intermedia . .	826	Persicaria . .	874	fruticosa . .	317
lanceolata . .	828	*Raii* . . .	868	*maculata* . . .	316
major . . .	826	*Roberti* . . .	868	*mixta* . . .	313
maritima . . .	829	viviparum . .	871	*nemoralis* . . .	314
media . . .	827	Polypodium alpestre .	1278	*norvegica* . . .	315
Timbali . . .	828	*calcareum* . .	1279	procumbens . .	314
Platanthera bifolia .	1004	cambricum . .	1276	reptans . . .	313
Poa alpina . .	1245	Dryopteris . .	1279	rupestris . . .	319
angustifolia . .	1241	*flexile* . . .	1278	*salisburgensis* . .	316
annua . . .	1239	Phegopteris . .	1277	Sibbaldi . .	321
aquatica . . .	1232	*Robertianum* . .	1279	Tormentilla . .	314
Balfourii . . .	1243	vulgare . . .	1276	verna . . .	316
Borreri . . .	1235	Polypogon littoralis .	1179	Poterium *muricatum* .	326
bulbosa . . .	1246	monspeliensis . .	1178	*officinale* . .	325
cæsia . . .	1243	*Polistichum*		Sanguisorba . .	326
compressa . .	1240	*aculeatum* . .	1283	*Prenanthes muralis* .	586
distans . . .	1235	*Lonchitis* . .	1282	Primula *acaulis* . .	649
flexuosa . . .	1244	Populus alba . .	931	*elatior* . . .	648
fluitans . . .	1233	*canescens* . .	931	farinosa . . .	650
glauca . . .	1243	*fastigiata* . .	933	*officinalis* . .	648
kœleri . . .	1242	nigra . . .	933	*scotica* . . .	650
laxa . . .	1244	tremula . . .	932	*variabilis* . .	648
loliacea . . .	1238	Potamogeton		veris . . .	648
maritima . . .	1234	*acuminatus* . .	958	*vulgaris* . . .	649
minor . . .	1244	acutifolius . .	964	Prunella vulgaris .	793
montana . . .	1243	*compressus* . .	963	Prunus *Arium* . .	298
nemoralis . .	1243	crispus . . .	961	Cerasus . .	298
Parnellii . . .	1243	*cuspidatus* . .	964	communis . .	297
polynoda . . .	1240	*decipiens* . . .	958	*domestica* . .	297
pratensis . . .	1241	*densus* . . .	962	*insititia* . . .	297

INDEX. 331

	FIG.
Padus	299
spinosa	297
Psama arenaria	1183
baltica	1185
Pseudathyrium	
alpestre	1278
Pteris aquilina	1303
Pulicaria dysenterica	516
vulgaris	517
Pulmonaria	
angustifolia	692
officinalis	692
Pyrola arenaria	642
maritima	642
media	643
minor	644
rotundifolia	642
secunda	645
uniflora	641
Pyrus acerba	334
Achras	333
Aria	335
Aucuparia	337
Briggsii	333
communis	333
cordata	333
domestica	337
fennica	335
germanica	340
intermedia	335
latifolia	335
Malus	334
pinnatifida	335
Pyraster	333
rupicola	335
scandica	335
torminalis	336
Quercus intermedia	915
pedunculata	915
Robur	915
sessiliflora	915
Radiola linoides	193
Millegrana	193
Ranunculus acris	17
aquatilis	9
arvensis	23
auricomus	16
Bachii	9
Baudotii	9
Boraeanus	17
bulbosus	20
chaerophyllos	19
circinatus	9
coenosus	10
confervoides	9
confusus	9
divaricatus	9
diversifolius	9
Drouetii	9
Ficaria	14
fissifolius	9
Flammula	12
floribundus	9
fluitans	9
Godronii	9

	FIG.
hederaceus	10
heterophyllus	9
hirsutus	21
homophyllus	10
intermedius	10
Lenormandi	10
Lingua	11
marinus	9
ophioglossifolius	13
pantothryx	9
parviflorus	22
parvulus	21
peltatus	9
pencedanifolius	9
penicillatus	9
philonotis	21
pseudo-fluitans	9
radians	9
repens	18
reptans	12
salsuginosus	9
Sardous	21
sceleratus	15
tomophyllus	17
trichophyllus	9
tripartitus	10
triphyllos	9
truncatus	9
vulgaris	9
vulgatus	17
Raphanus maritimus	112
Raphanistrum	112
Reseda alba	115
fruticulosa	115
Hookeri	115
lutea	114
luteola	113
suffruticulosa	115
Rhamnus catharticus	224
Frangula	225
Rhinanthus	
angustifolius	768
Rhodiola rosea	360
Crista-gali	768
major	768
minor	768
Reichenbachii	768
Rhynchospora alba	1086
fusca	1085
Ribes alpinum	372
Grossularia	370
nigrum	373
petraeum	371
rubrum	371
sativum	371
spicatum	371
sylvestre	371
Uva-crispa	370
Roemeria hybrida	43
Romulea Columnae	1019
Rosa agrestis	33
Andevagensis	331
arvatica	331
arvensis	332
aspernata	331
Bakeri	331
bibracteata	332
Billietii	330
biserrata	331

	FIG.
Blondaeana	331
Borreri	331
bractescens	331
Briggsii	330
britannica	329
caesia	331
canescens	331
canina	331
celerata	331
coerulea	329
collina	331
concinna	331
coronata	329
coriifolia	331
Crepiniana	331
cryptopoda	330
decipiens	331
Doniana	329
dumalis	331
dumetorum	331
Eglanteria	330
farinosa	329
fastigiata	332
Forsteri	331
frondosa	331
gallicoides	332
glabra	329
glaucophylla	331
gracilescens	329
gracilis	329
Hailstonei	331
implexa	331
incana	331
inodora	330
involuta	329
Jundzilliana	329
Kosinciana	331
laevigata	329
leucochroa	332
lutetiana	331
marginata	331
micrantha	330
mollis	329
mollissima	329
monsoniae	332
monticola	331
Moorei	329
Nicholsoni	329
nivalis	329
nuda	331
obovata	329
obtusifolia	331
occidentalis	329
opaca	332
permixta	330
pimpinellifolia	328
platyphylla	331
pomifera	329
pruinosa	331
Pseudo-rubiginosa	329
pulverulenta	330
repens	332
Reuteri	331
Robertsoni	329
rubella	330
rubiginosa	330
Sabini	329
sarmentacea	331
scabriuscula	329

	FIG.		FIG.		FIG.
sclerophylla	231	Idæus	306	*maximus*	859
scuticosa	331	*imbricatus*	307	*nemorosus*	861
sepium	330	*incurvatus*	307	obtusifolius	858
Sherrardi.	329	*infestus*	307	*palustris*	863
Smithii	329	*intermedius*	308	*pratensis*.	857
sphærica	331	*Kœhleri*	307	pulcher	862
spinonissima	328	*latifolius*	307	*rupestris*	860
stylosa	332	*Leesii*	306	sanguineus	861
subcristata	331	*Leightoni.*	307	*Steinii*	863
subglobosa	329	*Leightonianus*	307	*sylvestris*	858
surculosa	331	*Lejeunii*	307	*viridis*	861
sylvestris	329	*lentiginosus*	307	Ruppia maritima	955
sylvicola	330	*leucostachys*	307	*rostellata*	955
systyla	331	Lindleianus	307	*spiralis*	955
tomentella	331	*macrophyllus*	307	Ruscus aculeatus	1034
tomentosa	329	*mucronatus*	307		
uncinella	331	*mucronulatus*	307		
urbica	331	*mutabilis*	307	Sagina *ambigua*	146
verticillocanthu	331	*nemorosus*	307	*apetala*	146
villosa	329	*nitidus*	307	*ciliata*	146
vinacea	331	*obliquus*	307	*debilis*	146
Watsoni	331	*pallidus*	307	*densa*	146
Wilsoni	329	*pampinosus*	307	Linæi	147
Woodsiana	329	*plicatus*	307	*maritima*	146
Rubia peregrina	468	*præruptorum*	307	*nivalis*	147
tinctoria	468	*Pseudo-idæcus*	308	nodosa	148
Rubus *abruptus*	307	*Purchasii.*	307	procumbens	146
adscitus	307	*purpureus*	307	*saxatilis*	147
affinis	307	*pygmæus*	307	*subulata*	147
althæifolius	307	*pyramidalis*	307	Sagittaria sagittifolia	968
amplificatus	307	*Radula*	307	Salicornia herbacea	837
Babingtonii	307	*ramosus*	307	*lignosa*	837
Balfourianus	307	*Reuteri*	307	*megastachya*	837
Bellardi	307	*rhamnifolius*	307	*procumbens*	837
Bloxami	307	*rosaceus*	307	Salix *acuminata*	921
Borreri	307	*rotundifolius*	307	*acutifolia.*	924
Briggsii	307	*rubicolor*	308	alba	918
cæsius	308	*rudis*	307	*ambigua*	925
calvatus	307	Salteri	307	amygdalina	919
carpinifolius	307	*Saltuum*	307	*Andersoniana*	924
cavatifolius	307	saxatilis	309	*aquatica*	922
Chamæmorus	310	*scaber*	307	*Arbuscula*	928
Colemanni	307	*Schlechtendahlii*	307	*arbutifolia*	928
concinnus	307	Sprengelii	307	*arenaria*	925
conjungens	307	*suberectus*	307	*argentea*	925
cordifolius	307	*sublustris*	307	*ascendens*	925
corylifolius	307	*tenuis*	308	aurita	923
dentatus	307	*thyrsoideus*	307	*bicolor*	924
denticulatus	307	*tuberculatus*	307	*Barreriana*	924
derasus	307	*ulmifolius*	308	*cærulea*	918
discolor	308	*umbrosus*	307	Caprea	922
diversifolius	307	*vestitus*	307	*carinata*	928
dumetorum	307	*villicaulis*	307	*cinerea*	922
Emerstistylus	307	*vulgaris*	307	*contorta*	919
fastigiatus	307	*Wahlbergii*	307	*cotinifolia*	924
fissus	307	Rumex Acetosa	864	*Croweana*	924
foliosus	307	Acetosella	865	*cuspidata*	916
fruticosus	307	*acutus*	857	*damascena*	924
fusco-ater	307	*alpinus*	856	*daphnoides*	924
fuscus	307	aquaticus	856	*Davalliana*	924
glandulosus	307	conglomeratus	860	*decipiens*	917
Grabowskii	307	*conspersus*	857	*Dicksoniana*	924
Guntheri	307	crispus	857	*Doniana*	920
hemistemon	307	*elongatus*	857	*ferruginea*	921
hirtus	307	*Friesii*	858	*floribunda*	924
hirtifolius	307	Hydrolapathum	859	*foetida*	925
hirpidus	308	*Knafi*	863	*Forbyana*	920
humifusus	307	*longifolius*	856	*Forsteriana*	924
Hystrix	307	maritimus	863	fragilis	917

INDEX.

	PAG.
fusca	925
glauca	926
Grahami	928
Helix	920
herbacea	930
hirta	924
Hoffmanniana	919
holosericea	921
incubacea	925
lævis	928
Lambertiana	920
lanata	927
lanceolata	919
Laponum	926
laurina	924
laxiflora	924
livida	928
Meyeriana	916
mollissima	921
Myrsinites	928
myrtilloides	924
nigricans	924
nitens	924
oleifolia	922
parvifolia	925
pentandra	916
phylicifolia	924
petræa	924
phillyreæfolia	924
pontederana	920
propinqua	924
procumbens	928
prostrata	925
prunifolia	928
purpurea	920
radicans	924
ramulosa	220
repens	925
reticulata	929
rosmarinifolia	925
rubra	920
rugosa	921
rupestris	924
Russelliana	917
Sadleri	928
serrata	928
Smithiana	921
stipularis	924
spathulata	922
sphacelata	922
Stuartiana	926
tenuifolia	924
tenuior	924
tetrapla	924
Trevirani	919
triandra	919
undulata	919
vacciniifolia	928
venulosa	928
versifolia	925
viminalis	921
viridis	917
vitellina	918
Weigeliana	924
Woolgariana	920
Wulfeniana	924
Salsola Kali	840
Salvia clandestina	775
pratensis	775

	PAG.
Verbenaca	776
Sambucus Ebulus	461
nigra	460
Samolus Valerandi	661
Sanguisorba officinalis	325
Sanicula europæa	397
Saponaria hybrida	132
officinalis	132
Sarothamnus scoparius	231
Saussurea alpina	555
Saxifraga affinis	377
aizoides	375
autumnalis	375
cæspitosa	378
cernua	380
decipiens	377
elegans	385
elongata	377
Geum	386
gracilis	385
granulata	379
greenlandica	378
hibernica	377
Hirculus	376
hirsuta	385
hirta	377
hypnoides	377
incurvifolia	378
læte-virens	377
lævis	377
leptophylla	377
nivalis	383
oppositifolia	374
palmata	377
platypetala	377
punctata	385
quinquefida	377
rivularis	381
serratifolia	385
sponhemica	377
stellaris	384
Sternbergii	377
tridactylites	382
trifida	377
umbrosa	385
Scabiosa arvensis	494
Columbaria	493
succisa	492
Scandix Anthriscus	444
cerefolium	443
Pecten	439
Scheuchzeria palustris	973
Schoberia fruticosa	838
maritima	839
Schœnus nigricans	1083
Scilla autumnalis	1043
nutans	1044
verna	1042
Scirpus acicularis	1089
cæspitosus	1094
caricinus	1087
Caricis	1087
carinatus	1101
Davalii	1101
fluitans	1095
glaucus	1101
Holoschœnus	1098
lacustris	1101
maritimus	1102

	PAG.
multicaulis	1092
palustris	1091
parvulus	1090
pauciflorus	1093
planifolius	1087
pungens	1099
pygmæus	1097
riparius	1097
Rothii	1099
rufus	1088
Savii	1097
setaceus	1096
sylvaticus	1103
Tabernæmontani	1101
triqueter	1100
Scleranthus annuus	835
biennis	835
perennis	836
Sclerochloa Borreri	1235
conferta	1235
distans	1235
loliacea	1238
maritima	1234
multicaulis	1235
procumbens	1236
rigida	1237
Scolopendrium vulgare	1300
Scrophularia aquatica	741
Balbisii	741
cinerea	741
Ehrharti	741
nodosa	740
Scorodonia	742
umbrosa	741
vernalis	743
Scutellaria galericulata	794
minor	795
Sedum acre	366
albescens	368
album	364
anglicum	362
dasyphyllum	363
elegans	368
Fabaria	361
Forsterianum	368
glaucum	368
micranthum	364
pruinatum	368
purpurascens	361
reflexum	368
Rhodiola	360
rupestre	368
sexangulare	367
Telephium	361
teretifolium	364
villosum	365
Selaginella selaginoides	1260
spinosa	1260
Sempervivum tectorum	369
Senebiera Coronopus	107
didyma	108
Senecio aquaticus	544
barbareæfolius	544
campestris	550
erucifolius	546
flosculosus	545
Jacobæa	545
lividus	542
maritima	550

	FIG.
paludosus	547
palustris	549
saracenicus	548
spathulæfolius	550
squalidus	543
sylvaticus	542
tenuifolius	546
viscosus	541
vulgaris	540
Serrafalcus arvensis	1220
Serratula tinctoria	554
Seseli Libanotis	427
Sesleria cærulea	1253
Setaria glauca	1160
verticillata	1159
viridis	1161
Sherardia arvensis	481
Sibbaldia procumbens	321
Sibthorpia europæa	746
Silaus pratensis	429
Silene acaulis	133
anglica	137
conica	138
Cucubalus	134
gallica	137
inflata	134
maritima	134
noctiflora	139
nutans	136
Otites	135
paradoxa	136
quinquevulnera	137
Silybum mariamum	556
Simethis bicolor	1055
planifolia	1055
Sinapis alba	80
arvensis	81
Cheiranthus	77
incana	83
nigra	82
tenuifolia	75
Sison Amomum	405
Sisymbrium alliaria	72
Irio	70
murale	76
officinale	69
polyceratium	72
Sophia	71
tenuifolium	75
Thaliana	60
Sisyrinchium	
angustifolium	1018
bermudiana	1018
Sium angustifolium	414
erectum	414
latifolium	413
repens	403
Smilacina bifolia	1032
Smyrnium Olusatrum	453
Solanum Dulcamara	713
luteo-virescens	714
miniatum	714
nigrum	714
Solidago cambrica	501
Virga-aurea	501
Sonchus alpinus	589
arvensis	590
asper	592
cœruleus	589

	FIG.
oleraceus	592
palustris	591
Sorbus fennica	335
latifolia	335
scandica	335
Sparganium affine	940
minimum	941
natans	940
ramosum	939
simplex	940
Spartina alterniflora	1201
stricta	1201
Townsendii	1201
Spartium scoparium	231
Specularia hybrida	623
Spergula arvensis	171
nodosa	148
saginoides	147
sativa	171
stricta	151
subulata	147
vulgaris	171
Spergularia marina	170
media	170
rubra	170
rupestris	170
salina	170
Spiræa Filipendula	302
salicifolia	300
Ulmaria	301
Spiranthes æstivalis	992
autumnalis	991
cernua	993
gemmipara	993
Romanzoviana	993
Stachys ambigua	801
arvensis	802
Betonica	798
germanica	799
palustris	801
sylvatica	800
Statice Armeria	824
bahusiensis	821
Behen	821
auriculæfolia	822
bellidifolia	823
binervosa	822
Caspia	822
Dodartii	822
Limonium	821
occidentalis	822
oxylepis	822
rariflora	821
reticulata	823
serotina	821
spathulata	822
Stellaria aquatica	163
Boræana	165
cerastoides	162
Elizabethæ	165
glauca	168
graminea	167
Holostea	169
media	165
neglecta	165
nemorum	164
palustris	168
scapigera	167
uliginosa	166

	FIG.
umbrosa	165
Stratiotes aloides	978
Sturmia Loeselii	980
minima	1176
Suæda fruticosa	838
maritima	839
Subularia aquatica	94
Symphytum officinale	705
patens	705
tuberosum	706
Tamarix anglica	175
gallica	175
Tamus communis	1026
Tanacetum vulgare	535
Taraxacum Dens-leonis	593
erythrospermum	593
lævigatum	593
officinale	593
palustre	593
Taxus baccata	936
fastigiata	936
Teesdalia Iberis	98
nudicaulis	98
Teucrium Botrys	815
Chamædrys	816
scordioides	814
Scordium	814
Scorodonia	813
Thalictrum alpinum	2
calcareum	3
flavum	4
flexuosum	3
Kochii	3
majus	3
minus	3
montanum	3
Morisonii	4
riparium	4
saxatile	3
sphærocarpum	4
Thesium divaricatum	881
humifusum	881
linophyllum	881
Thlaspi alpestre	97
arvense	95
occitanum	97
perfoliatum	96
sylvestre	97
virens	97
Thrincia hirta	582
Thymus Acinos	788
Chamædrys	786
Serpyllum	786
Tilia europæa	200
grandifolia	200
intermedia	200
parviflora	200
platyphyllos	200
vulgaris	200
Tillæa muscosa	358
Tinia cylindracea	1006
Tofieldia borealis	1056
palustris	1056
Tordylium maximum	438
Torilis Anthriscus	446
infesta	447
nodosa	445

INDEX. 335

	FIG.
Tormentilla erecta	314
officinalis.	314
reptans	314
Tragopogon *grandiflora*	576
minor	576
porrifolius	577
pratensis	576
Trichomanes *Andrewsii*	1308
brevisetum	1308
radicans	1308
speciosum.	1308
Trichonema	
bulbocodium	1019
Columnæ	1019
Trientalis europæa	656
Trifolium arvense	246
Bocconi	245
dubium	263
elegans	254
filiforme	264
fragiferum	259
glomeratum	255
hybridum	261
incarnatum	244
maritimum	251
medium	250
minus	263
Molinerii.	244
ochroleucum	248
ornithopedioides	243
pratense	249
procumbens	262
repens	260
resupinatum	257
scabrum	253
stellatum.	247
striatum	252
strictum	254
subterraneum	258
suffocatum	256
Triglochin maritimum	975
palustre	974
Trigonella	
ornithopodioides	243
Trinia vulgaris	406
Triodia decumbens	1251
Trisetum flavescens	1196
Triticum acutum	1209
alpinum	1209
caninum	1210
junceum	1209
laxum	1209
littorale	1209
loliaceum.	1223
pungens	1209
repens	1209
Trollius europæus	25
Tulipa sylvestris	1036
Turritis glabra	56
hirsuta	58
Tussilago Farfara	538
hybrida	539
Petasites	539
Typha angustifolia	938
latifolia	937
media	937
Udora canadensis	976

	FIG.
Ulex europæus	226
Gallii	227
nanus	227
strictus	226
Ulmus campestris	907
campestris	906
carpinifolia	907
glabra	907
major	906
montana	906
stricta	907
suberosa	907
Urtica dioica	903
Dodartii	902
pilulifera	902
urens	901
Utricularia *Bremii*	666
intermedia	667
minor	666
neglecta	665
vulgaris	665
Vaccinium Myrtillus	624
Oxycoccos	627
uliginosum	625
Vitis-idæa	626
Valantia cruciata	409
Valeriana dioica	483
Locusta	486
micani	484
officinalis.	484
pyrenaica	485
sambucifolia	484
Valerianella Auricula	488
carinata	487
dentata	489
eriocarpa	489
mixta	489
Morisonii	489
olitoria	486
tridentata	488
Verbascum Blattaria	725
Lychnitis	728
nigrum	727
pulverulentum	729
Thapsus	724
virgatum	726
Verbena officinalis	820
Veronica agrestis	759
alpina	750
Anagallis	753
arvensis	761
Beccabunga	754
Buxbaumii	760
Chamædrys	757
eximia	761
hederæfolia	758
hirsuta	752
humifusa	751
hybrida	748
montana	756
officinalis.	752
polita	759
saligna	752
saxatilis	749
scutellata.	755
serpyllifolia	751
spicata	748

	FIG.
triphyllos.	763
verna	762
Viburnum Lantana	462
Opulus	463
Vicia *angustifolia*	284
bithynica	286
Bobartii	284
Cracca	279
gracilis	278
hirsuta	277
hybrida	283
lævigata	283
lathyroides	285
lutea	283
Orobus	281
sativa	284
segetalis	284
sepium	282
sylvatica	280
tetrasperma	278
Villarsia reniformis	682
nymphæoides	682
Vinca major	670
minor	671
Viola *arenaria*	123
arvensis	125
calcarea	122
canina	124
Curtisii	125
flavicornis	124
grandiflora	125
hirta	122
lactea	124
lutea	125
odorata	121
palustris	120
permixta	121
persicæfolia	124
pumila	124
Reichenbachiana	124
Riviniana	124
sabulosa	125
sepincola	121
stagnina	124
sylvatica	124
tricolor	125
Viscum album	456
Vulpia membranacea	1226
Wahlenbergia	
hederacia	622
Woodsia *hyperborea*	1307
ilvensis	1307
Wolffia arrhiza	918
Xanthium Strumarium	518
Zannichellia	
brachystemon	954
macrostemon	954
major	954
palustris	954
pedicellata	954
pedunculata	954
polycarpa	954
tenuissima	954
Zostera marina	949
nana	950

INDEX.

OF

ENGLISH AND POPULAR NAMES.

Name	FIG.	Name	FIG.	Name	FIG.
Absinth	537	Andromeda, Marsh	631	Barberry	33
Aceras, Man	1009	Anemone, Pasque	5	Barley, Meadow	1206
Achillea, Milfoil	531	Wood	6	Sea	1208
Sneezewort	530	Angelica, Wild	432	Wall	1207
Aconite	30	Antennaria, Mountain	510	Wood	1205
Acorus, Sweet	943	Pearl	511	Bartsia, Alpine	764
Adder's tongue	1273	Anthoxanth, Sweet	1164	Red	766
Adiant, Maidenhair	1304	Anthyllis	267	Viscid	765
Adonis	7	Apium, Celery	402	Basil	790
Æthusa	425	Lesser	404	Bastard-balm	796
Agrimony, Common	327	Procumbent	403	Beaksedge, Brown	1085
Hemp	495	Apple, Wild or Crab	334	White	1086
Agropyrum, Couch	1209	Arbutus	628	Beam, White	335
Fibrous	1210	Archangel, Yellow	812	Bearberry, Black	630
Agrostis, Bristle	1182	Arnoseris, Dwarf	608	Common	629
Brown	1181	Arrow-grass	974	Beardgrass, Annual	1178
Common	1180	Arrowhead	968	Perennial	1179
Silky	1183	Artimisia, Common	536	Bear's-foot	26
Aira, Early	1192	Field	534	Bedstraw, Ladies'	470
Grey	1191	Sea	535	Beech	914
Silvery	1193	Wormwood	537	Beech Fern	1277
Tufted	1189	Arum	942	Beet	850
Wavy	1190	Asarabacca	882	Belladonna	715
Alchemil, Alpine	323	Asarum	882	Betony	798
Common	322	Ash, Common	668	Bidens, Nodding	519
Field	324	Mountain	337	Three-cleft	520
Alder, Common	909	Asparagus	1033	Bilberry	624
Berry-bearing	224	Aspen	932	Bindweed, Black	869
Alexanders	453	Asperugo German	708	Small	684
Alisma, Common	969	Asperule, Small	480	Birch, Common	910
Floating	971	Woodruff	479	Dwarf	911
Lesser	970	Asphodel, Bog	1055	Bird's-foot, Common	274
Alkanet, Common	702	Lancashire	1055	Sand	273
Green	703	Scottish	1056	Trefoil	265
Allgood	849	Aster, Goldilocks	497	Bird's-nest, Orchis	989
All-heal	484	Sea	496	Yellow	646
Alliara, Common	72	Astragal, Alpine	269	Bishopweed	407
Allium, Broad	1052	Purple	268	Bistort	872
Chive	1049	Sweet	270	Bittercress, Bulbiferous	67
Crow	1051	Astrantia, Larger	398	Hairy	66
Field	1048	Atropa, Deadly	715	Large	63
Large	1046	Avens, Common	304	Meadow	64
Round-headed	1050	Water	305	Narrow-leaved	65
Sand	1047	Awlwort, Water	94	Bittersweet	713
Triquetrous	1053			Blackberry	307
Allosorus, Curled	1280	Baldmoney	430	Blackthorn	297
Allseed	193	Ballota, Black	806	Bladderfern, Brittle	1305
Althæa, Hispid	199	Balm, bastard	796	Mountain	1306
Marsh	198	Balsam, Orange	219	Bladder-seed	452
Alyssum, Small	86	Yellow	218	Bladderwort, Common	665
Sweet	87	Baneberry	31	Intermediate	667

INDEX. 337

	FIG.		FIG.		FIG.
Bladderwort, Lesser	666	Burvet, Garden	326	Carex, Pendulous	1151
Bleaberry	624	Great	325	Pile-headed	1135
Blechnum, Hard	1302	Salad	326	Prickly	1121
Blinks	174	Saxifrage	415	Remote	1117
Bluebell	1044	Burweed, Broad	518	Rock	1110
Blueberry	624	Butcher's Broom	1034	Russet	1125
Bluebottle	572	Butterbur	539	Sand	1122
Blue-eyed Grass	1018	Buttercup	17	Slender	1137
Blysmus, Broad	1087	Butterwort, Alpine	662	Star-headed	1115
Narrow	1088	Common	662	Thin-spiked	1149
Bog-rush	1083	Pale	664	Tufted	1126
Borage	707	Butome, Common	967	Vernal	1133
Borecole	78			Whitish	1116
Box	897	Cabbage, St. Patrick's	385	Wood	1148
Brake or Bracken	1303	Calamint, Common	789	Yellow	1141
Rock	1280	Field	788	Carline thistle	569
Bramble	307	Hedge	790	Carnation	131
Brandy-bottle	35	Caltha, Marsh	24	Carrot	450
Brassica, Black	82	Cameline	93	Carum, Caraway	411
Cabbage	78	Campanula, Clustered	615	Corn	409
Charlock	81	Corn	623	Parsley	408
Field	79	Creeping	618	Tuberous	412
Hoary	83	Giant	617	Whorled	410
Isle of Man	77	Harebell	621	Catabrose, Water	1247
Mustard	80	Ivy	622	Catchfly, Nottingham	136
Sand	76	Nettle-leaved	616	Catmint	792
Wall	75	Rampion	619	Cat's-ear	510, 584
Broccoli	78	Spreading	620	Cat's-tail	937, 1167
Brome, Barren	1217	Campion, Bladder	134	Caucalis, Broad	449
Compact	1219	Moss	133	Knotted	445
Field	1220	Red	141	Small	448
Great	1218	White	140	Spreading	447
Hairy	1216	Canary-grass	1165	Upright	446
Tall	1221	Candytuft, Bitter	99	Cauliflower	78
Upright	1215	Caper-spurge	890	Celandine, Common	42
Brooklime	754	Capsell	101	Lesser	14
Brookweed	661	Caraway	411	Celery	402
Broom, Butcher's	1034	Carex, Acute	1127	Centaurea, Black	570
Common	231	Alpine	1128	Corn	572
Broomrape, Blue	721	Axillary	1118	Greater	571
Branched	722	Black	1130	Jersey	573
Clove-scented	717	Bladder	1153	Star-thistle	574
Great	716	Bottle	1152	Yellow	575
Lesser	720	Buxbaum's	1129	Centaury	674
Red	718	Capillary	1145	Centranth, Red	482
Tall	719	Carnation	1144	Centuncle, Small	660
Brussels sprouts	78	Curved	1124	Cephalanthera, Large	984
Bryony, Black	1026	Cyperus-like	1150	Narrow	985
Common	357	Dioecious	1108	Red	986
Buckbean	681	Distant	1142	Cerast, Alpine	161
Buckthorn, Alder	225	Divided	1123	Common	159
Common	224	Dotted	1143	Field	160
Sea	880	Downy	1136	Starwort	162
Buckwheat, Climbing	869	Dwarf	1131	Ceratophyll	899
Bugle, Creeping	817	Elongated	1114	Ceterach, Scaly	1301
Erect	818	Few-flowered	1111	Chaffweed	660
Yellow	819	Fingered	1132	Chamagrostis, Dwarf	1176
Bugloss, Small	704	Flea	1109	Chamomile, Common	528
Viper's	690	Fox	1120	Corn	527
Bullace	333	Glaucous	1147	Fetid	526
Bulrush	1101	Hairy	1138	Wild	525
Buplever, Falcate	420	Hare's-foot	1113	Yellow	529
Hare's-ear	417	Longbracted	1140	Charlock	81
Narrow	418	Marsh	1154	Jointed	112
Slender	419	Mountain	1134	White	112
Burdock, Common	553	Mud	1146	Cherleria, Mossy	149
Bur-Marigold	519	Oval	1112	Cherry, Dwarf or Wild	298
Parsley	448	Pale	1139	Bird	299
-reed	939	Panicled	1119	Chervil, Burr	444

		FIG.
Grass, Fiorin	.	. 1180
Foxtail	.	1172—1175
Hair	.	. 1193
Hare's-tail	.	. 1177
Holy	.	. 1163
Lyme	.	. 1204
Manna	.	1232—1237
Marram	.	. 1185
Meadow	.	1238—1246
Millet	.	. 1156
Nit	.	. 1184
Parnassus		. 389
Quaking	.	.1230, 1231
Quitch	.	. 1209
Rye	.	. 1211
Scorpion	.	697—701
Squirrel-tailed		. 1208
Timothy	.	. 1167
Vernal	.	. 1164
-wrack	.	. 949
Great Burnet	.	. 325
Great Willow-herb	.	342
Greek Valerian	.	. 683
Greenwood	.	. 228
Gromwell, Common	.	695
Corn	.	. 694
Ground-Ivy	.	. 791
Pine	.	. 819
Groundsel	.	. 540
Guelder-Rose	.	. 463
Guimauve	.	. 198
Habenaria, Butterfly	.	1004
Dense-spiked	.	. 1006
Fragrant	.	. 1005
Green	.	. 1008
Small	.	. 1007
Hair-grass	.	. 1193
Hardheads	.	. 570
Harebell	.	. 621
Hare's Ear	.	74, 417
Hare's-tail, Ovate	.	1177
Hart's-tongue	.	. 1300
Hartwort, Great	.	. 438
Hawkbit, Autumnal	.	. 581
Common	.	. 580
Lesser	.	. 582
Hawk's-beard	.	594—599
Hawkweed, Alpine	.	. 601
Honeywort	.	. 603
Mouse-ear	.	. 600
Prenanth	.	. 606
Savoy	.	. 605
Umbellate	.	. 604
Wall	.	. 602
Hawthorn	.	. 338
Hazel	.	. 913
Heartsease	.	. 125
Heath, Ciliated	.	. 637
Cornish	.	. 639
Cross-leaved	.	. 636
Mediterranean	.	. 638
Scotch	.	. 635
St. Dabeoc's	.	. 633
Heather, Common	.	. 640
Scotch	.	. 635
Hedge Mustard	.	. 69
Hellebore, Fetid	.	. 27
Green	.	. 26

		FIG.
Helleborine	.	982, 983
Helminth, Oxtongue	.	578
Hemlock, Common	.	451
Water	.	. 401
Hemp Agrimony	.	495
Nettle	.	. 805
Henbane	.	. 712
Henbit	.	. 808
Heracleum	.	. 437
Herb-Bennet	.	. 304
Herb, Christopher	.	31
Gerard	.	. 407
Paris	.	. 1027
Robert	.	. 206
Herminium, Musk	.	1010
Herniary	.	. 633
Hesperis	.	. 68
Hippocrepis	.	. 275
Hippophæ	.	. 880
Hog's Fennel	.	. 433
Hogweed	.	. 437
Holcus, Common	.	1198
Soft	.	. 1199
Holly	.	. 222
Sea	.	. 399
Holosteum, Umbellate		158
Holygrass, Northern	.	1163
Honewort	.	. 406
Honeysuckle, Common		464
Fly	.	. 466
Perfoliate	.	. 465
Hop	.	. 905
Horehound, Black	.	806
White	.	. 797
Hornbeam	.	. 912
Horned pondweed	.	954
Poppy	.	. 44
Hornwort	.	. 899
Horseradish	.	. 84
Horsetail	.	. 1264
Hottonia, Water	.	647
Hound's Tongue,		
Common	.	. 709
Green	.	. 710
Houseleek	.	. 369
Hutchinsia, Rock	.	100
Hyacinth, Grape	.	1045
Wild	.	. 1044
Hydrocotyle, Common		396
Hymenophyll, Tunbridge		
		1309
Hypericum, Common	.	180
Flax-leaved	.	. 184
Hairy	.	. 186
Imperforate	.	. 181
Large-flowered	.	. 178
Marsh	.	. 188
Mountain	.	. 187
Slender	.	. 185
Square-stalked	.	. 182
Trailing	.	. 183
Tutsan	.	. 179
Hypochœre, Glabrous		583
Long-rooted	.	. 584
Spotted	.	. 585
Illecebrum, Whorled	.	834
Inule, Common	.	. 516

		FIG.
Inule, Elecampane	.	512
Rigid	.	. 515
Samphire	.	. 514
Small	.	. 517
Willow-leaved	.	. 513
Iris, Fetid	.	. 1016
Yellow	.	. 1015
Ivy, Common	.	. 455
Ground	.	. 791
Jack-by-the-hedge	.	72
Jacob's Ladder	.	. 683
Jasione, Sheep's-bit	.	612
Juniper	.	. 935
Kail, Scotch	.	. 78
Kidney Vetch	.	. 267
Knapweed	.	. 570
Knawel	.	. 835
Knotgrass	.	. 867
Kobresia, Sedge-like	.	1107
Kœleria, Crested	.	1252
Lady's Bedstraw	.	470
Fingers	.	. 267
Mantle	.	. 322
Slipper	.	. 1014
Smock	.	. 64
Tresses	.	. 991
Lamb's-lettuce	.	. 486
Succory	.	. 608
Lamium, Henbit	.	808
Red	.	. 809
Spotted	.	. 811
White	.	. 810
Yellow	.	. 812
Lapsane	.	. 609
Larkspur,	.	. 29
Lathræa	.	. 723
Laurel, Spurge	.	. 879
Lavatera, Sea	.	. 194
Lavender, Sea	.	. 821
Leek, Sand	.	. 1047
Wild	.	. 1046
Leersia	.	. 1155
Lent Lily	.	. 1022
Leonurus, Motherwort		807
Leopard's-bane	.	. 551
Lepturus, Curved	.	1202
Lettuce, Alpine	.	. 589
Prickly	.	. 587
Wall	.	. 586
Willow	.	. 588
Lily, Lent	.	. 1022
Lily-of-the-Valley	.	1031
Lime-tree	.	. 200
Limnanth	.	. 682
Limosel	.	. 745
Linaria, Common	.	732
Ivy	.	. 737
Lesser	.	. 736
Pale	.	. 733
Pellisser's	.	. 734
Pointed	.	. 739
Round-leaved	.	. 738
Supine	.	. 735

INDEX. 341

	FIG.
Ling	640
Linnæa, Northern	467
Linseed	189
Liparis, Two-leaved	980
Listera, Heart-leaved	988
Twayblade	987
Lithosperm, Common	695
Corn	694
Creeping	696
Littorel	831
Livelong	361
Lloydia, Mountain	1037
Lobelia, Acrid	611
Water	610
Loiseleuria, Trailing	632
Lolium, Darnel	1212
Ryegrass	1211
London Pride	385
London Rocket	70
Loosestrife	652
Loosestrife, Purple	354
Lords-and-Ladies	942
Lotus, Common	265
Slender	266
Lousewort	770
Lovage, Scotch	428
Lucern	235
Ludwigia, Marsh	351
Lungwort	692
Lychnis, Alpine	145
Corn	142
Meadow	143
Red	140
White	140
Viscid	144
Lycopus	777
Lymegrass, Sand	1204
Lysimachia, Common	652
Moneywort	654
Tufted	653
Wood	655
Lythrum, Hyssop	355
Spiked	354
Madder, Field	481
Wild	468
Madwort	703
Maianthemum, Two-leaved	1032
Maiden-hair	1304
Malaxis, Bog	979
Male Fluellen	738, 739
Mallow, Common	196
Dwarf	195
Marsh	198
Musk	197
Tree	194
Maple, Common	220
Great	221
Sycamore	221
Maram, Sea	1165
Marestail	395
Marigold, Bur	519
Corn	522
Marsh	24
Marjoram, Wild	787
Marram-grass	1155
Masterwort	435

	FIG.
Matgrass	1203
Matricary, Common	525
Scentless	524
Matweed, Sea	1185
May	338
May-lily	1032
Mayweed, Stink	526
Maywort	469
Meadow Rue	4
Saffron	1057
Sweet	301
Medick, Black	236
Bur	239
Denticulate	237
Lucern	235
Purple	235
Sickle	234
Spotted	238
Medlar	340
Melampyre, Common	773
Crested	771
Purple	772
Small-flowered	774
Melick, Mountain	1249
Wood	1250
Melilot, Common	240
Field	241
White	242
Melittis, Balm	796
Menziesia, Blue	634
St. Dabeoc's	633
Mercury, Annual	896
Dog's	895
Perennial	895
Mertensia, Sea	693
Meu	430
Mezereon	878
Midsummer-men	360
Mignonette, Cut-leaved	114
Dyer's	113
White	115
Milfoil	531
Milfoil, Water	393
Whorled	394
Milium, Spreading	1156
Milk-thistle	556
Milkvetch	270
Milkwort, Common	126
Sea	657
Millet-grass	1156
Mimulus, Yellow	744
Mint, Bergamos	782
Cat	792
Corn	784
Horse	778
Pennyroyal	785
Pepper	781
Round-leaved	779
Spear	780
Water	782
Whorled	783
Mistletoe	456
Mithridate Mustard	95
Pepperwort	102
Mœnchia, Upright	157
Molinia, Purple	1248
Moneywort	654
Monkshood	30
Monk's Rhubarb	856

	FIG.
Monotrope	646
Montia, Water	174
Moonwort	1274
Moscatel, Tuberous	459
Moss Campion	133
Motherwort	807
Mountain-Ash	337
Mouse-ear Chickweed	159
Mousetail, Common	8
Mudwort	745
Mugwort	536
Mullein, Dark	727
Great	724
Hoary	729
Moth	725
Twiggy	726
White	728
Muscari, Grape	1045
Musk Thistle	557
Mustard, Black	82
Cultivated	80
Garlick	72
Hedge	69
Mithridate	95
Treacle	73
Tower	56
White	80
Wild	81
Myosote, Changing	701
Early	700
Field	699
Water	697
Wood	698
Myriophyl, Spiked	393
Whorled	394
Naiad, Grassy	953
Holly-leaved	952
Slender	951
Narcethium, Bog	1055
Narcissus, Daffodil	1022
Two-flowered	1023
Nard, Common	1203
Navelwort	359
Neottia, Bird's-nest	989
Nepeta, Catmint	792
Ground-Ivy	791
Nettle, Common	903
Dead	810
Roman	902
Small	901
Nightshade	713
Deadly	715
Enchanter's	352
Nipplewort	609
Nitgrass, Awned	1184
None-so-pretty	385
Nonsuch	236
Nottingham Catchfly	136
Nut	913
Nymphæa, White	34
Oak, British	915
Fern	1279
Oat. Perennial	1195
Wild	1194
Yellow	1196

INDEX.

	FIG.
Œnanth, Common	421
Fine-leaved	424
Hemlock	423
Parsley	422
Œnothera	350
Old Man's Beard	1
Ononis Restharrow	232
Small	233
Onopord, Common	568
Ophrys, Bee	1011
Fly	1013
Spider	1012
Opium, Poppy	36
Orache, Common	854
Frosted	855
Garden	853
Lesser Shrubby	851
Purslane	851
Stalked	852
Orchis, Bee	1011
Bird's-nest	989
Boy	979
Butterfly	1004
Dark-winged	997
Dwarf	997
Early	998
Fen	980
Fly	1013
Fragrant	1005
Frog	1008
Green-winged	995
Lizard	1002
Loose	999
Man	1009
Marsh	1001
Military	996
Musk	1010
Purple	998
Pyramidal	1003
Spider	1012
Spotted	1000
Ornithogalum, Common	1039
Drooping	1040
Spiked	1041
Orpine	361
Osier, Common	921
Purple	920
Osmund, Royal	1275
Oxalis, Procumbent	217
Sorrel	216
Oxeye Daisy	521
Oxlip	649
Oxtongue	578
Oxyrea, Kidney	866
Oxytrope, Purple	272
Yellow	271
Paddock-pipes	1267
Pæony	32
Paigle	649
Panicum, Cockspur	1162
Fingered	1157
Glabrous	1158
Glaucous	1160
Green	1161
Rough	1159
Pansy, Field	125

	FIG.
Paris	1027
Parnassia, Marsh	389
Parsley, Bastard Stone	405
Beaked	444
Bur	448
Common	408
Corn	409
Fern	1280
Fool's	425
Hedge	446
Milk	434
Piert	324
Parsnip, Common	436
Cow	437
Water	413
Pasque-flower	5
Pea, Black	296
Earth Nut	291
Everlasting	292
Grass	287
Marsh	293
Meadow	290
Sea	294
Rough	289
Tuberous	295
Yellow	288
Pearlwort, Alpine	147
Knotted	148
Procumbent	146
Pear-tree	333
Pedicularis, Common	770
Marsh	769
Pellitory, Wall	904
Pennycress, Alpine	97
Field	95
Perfoliate	96
Penny-royal	785
Pennywort	359
Marsh	396
Peplis	356
Pepper-Saxifrage	429
Pepperwort, Mithridate	102
Periwinkle, Larger	670
Lesser	671
Persicaria, Common	874
Petty Whin	230
Pencedan, Broad	435
Marsh	434
Sea	433
Phalaris, Canary	1165
Pheasant's Eye	7
Phleum, Alpine	1168
Bœhmer's	1169
Rough	1170
Sand	1171
Timothy	1167
Physosperm, Cornish	452
Picris, Hawkweed	579
Pignut	441
Pilewort	14
Pillwort, Creeping	1262
Pimpernel, Bastard	660
Bog	659
Common	658
Scarlet	658
Yellow	655
Pimpinel, Common	415
Greater	416
Pine	934

	FIG.
Pine, Ground	819
Pink, Cheddar	131
Clove	131
Deptford	129
Maiden	130
Proliferous	128
Sea	824, 825
Wild	131
Pipewort	1080
Plane, Scotch	221
Plantain, Bucks-horn	830
Greater	826
Hoary	827
Ribwort	828
Sea	829
Water	969
Ploughman's Spikenard	515
Plum	297
Poa, Alpine	1245
Annual	1239
Bulbous	1246
Darnel	1238
Flattened	1240
Floating	1233
Hard	1237
Meadow	1241
Procumbent	1236
Reed	1232
Reflexed	1235
Roughish	1242
Sea	1234
Wavy	1244
Wood	1243
Polemonium, Blue	683
Polycarp, Four-leaved	172
Polygonum, Amphibious	873
Bistort	872
Climbing	869
Copse	870
Knotweed	867
Pale	875
Persicaria	874
Sea	868
Slender	877
Viviparous	874
Waterpepper	876
Polypody, Alpine	1278
Beech	1277
Common	1276
Oak	1279
Pondweed, Acute	964
Broad	956
Curly	961
Fennel	966
Horned	954
Long	959
Obtuse	963
Opposite	962
Perfoliate	960
Striving	958
Slender	965
Various-leaved	957
Poor man's weather-glass	658
Poplar, Aspen	932
Black	933
Grey	931
White	931

INDEX. 343

	FIG.		FIG.		FIG.
Poppy, Field	37	Ranunculus, Spear	12	Rush, Jointed	1062
Garden	36	Water	9	Obtuse	1063
Horned	44	Wood	16	Round-fruited	1064
Long-headed	38	Rape	79	Scouring	1270
Opium	36	Raspberry	306	Sea	1070
Pale	40	Rattle, Common	768	Sharp	1071
Rough	39	Red	769	Slender	1065
Sea	44	Reed	1254	Thread	1060
Welsh	41	Reedmace, Cat's-tail	937	Toad	1067
Potentil, Creeping	313	Great	937	Two-leaved	1074
Goose	318	Lesser	938	Wood	1075—1079
Hoary	315	Rest-harrow	232, 233		
Marsh	320	Rhubarb, Monk's	856		
Rock	319	Ribes, Black	373	Saffron, Meadow	1057
Shrubby	317	Currant	371	Sage, Meadow	775
Spring	316	Gooseberry	370	Wild	776
Strawberry-leaved	312	Mountain	372	Wood	813
Tormentil	314	Rib-grass	826	Sainfoin, Common	276
Potercum, Burnet	326	Ribwort	828	Salad Burnet	326
Prickwood	458	Roast-beef-plant	1016	Salicorn	837
Primrose, Bird's-eye	650	Robin, Ragged	143	Sallow	922
Common	648	Rock Braken	1280	Sallow-Thorn	880
Evening	350	Rockcist, Common	118	Salsify, Meadow	576
Mealy	650	Hoary	117	Purple	577
Peerless	1023	Spotted	116	Saltwort, Black	657
Privet	669	White	119	Prickly	840
Prunella	793	Rockcress, Bristol	61	Samole, Brookweed	661
Prunus, Birdcherry	299	Fringed	59	Samphire, Golden	514
Blackthorn	297	Glabrous	56	Marsh	837
Cherry	298	Hairy	58	Sea	431
Pteris, Brake	1303	Northern	62	Sandleek	1047
Purple Loosestrife	354	Thale	60	Sandspurry	170
Purslane, Sea	153, 851	Tower	57	Sandwort, Bog	151
Water	356	Rocket	75	Fine-leaved	152
Pyrus, Apple	334	Dyer's	113	Fringed	155
Beam	335	London	70	Ovate	153
Cut-leaved	336	Sea	110	Three-nerved	156
Pear	333	Yellow	51	Thyme-leaved	154
Rowan	337	Rock-rose	118	Vernal	150
		Rœmerea	43	Sanguisorb, Burnet	325
		Romulea	1019	Sanicle, Wood	397
Quakegrass, Common	1230	Rose-Bay	341	Saponaria	132
Lesser	1231	Burnet	328	Sauce-alone	72
Queen of the Meadows	301	Dog	331	Saussurea, Alpine	555
Queenstock	48	Downy	329	Savoy	78
Quilwort, European	1261	Field	332	Sawwort	554
Quitch Grass	1209	Scotch	328	Saxifrage, Alpine	383
		Sweetbriar	330	Brook	381
		Roseroot	360	Burnet	415
Radish, Wild	112	Rowan-tree	337	Cut-leaved	377
Ragged Robin	143	Rubus, Blackberry	307	Drooping	380
Ragwort	545	Cloudberry	310	Golden	387
Rampion, Garden	619	Dewberry	308	Kidney	386
Round-headed	613	Raspberry	306	London-pride	385
Spiked	614	Stone	309	Marsh	376
Ramps	619	Ruppia, Sea	955	Meadow	379
Ramsons	1052	Rupture-wort	833	Pepper	429
Ranunculus, Bulbous	20	Ruscus, Common	1034	Purple	374
Celery-leaved	15	Rush, Baltic	1061	Rue-leaved	382
Corn	23	Bog	1083	Star	384
Creeping	18	Capetate	1069	Tufted	378
Figwort	14	Chestnut	1073	Yellow	375
Fine-leaved	19	Common	1058	Scabious, Blue	492
Great	11	Dutch	1270	Field	494
Hairy	21	Dwarf	1068	Small	493
Ivy	10	Flowering	967	Scandix, Needle	439
Meadow	17	Hard	1059	Schœnus, Black	1083
Small-flowered	22	Heath	1066	Scheuchzeria, Marsh	973
Snaketongue	13	Highland	1072	Scirpus, Bristle	1096

	FIG.		FIG.		FIG.
Scirpus, Clustered	1098	Shieldfern, Holly	1282	Spleenwort, Lady	1290
Creeping	1091	Male	1286	Lanceolate	1292
Few-flowered	1093	Marsh	1284	Rock	1291
Floating	1095	Mountain	1285	Sea	1293
Lake	1101	Prickly	1283	Wallrue	1297
Many-stalked	1092	Rigid	1289	Spignel	430
Needle	1069	Shore weed	831	Spikenard,	
Savi's	1097	Sibbaldia, Procumbent	321	Ploughman's	515
Sea	1102	Sipthorpia, Common	746	Spindle-tree	223
Sharp	1099	Silaus, Meadow	429	Spiræa, Common	302
Small	1090	Silene, Bladder	134	Meadow	301
Triangular	1100	Dwarf	133	Willow	300
Tufted	1094	Night	139	Spiranth, Common	991
Wood	1103	Nodding	136	Drooping	993
Scleranth, Annual	835	Small-flowered	137	Summer	992
Perennial	836	Spanish	135	Spurge, Broad	885
Scorpion grass	697—701	Striated	138	Caper	890
Scotch Fir	934	Silver-weed	318	Dwarf	889
Scrophularia,		Simethis, Variegated	1054	Hairy	887
Balm-leaved	742	Sison, Hedge	405	Irish	886
Knotted	740	Sisymbrium, Broad	70	Laurel	879
Water	741	Common	69	Leafy	893
Yellow	743	Fine-leaved	71	Petty	888
Scurvy-grass	85	Sisyrinchium,		Portland	891
Sea-buckthorn	880	Narrow-leaved	1018	Purple	883
Heath	127	Sium, Broad	413	Sea	892
Holly	399	Lesser	414	Sun	884
Kale	111	Skullcap, Common	794	Wood	894
Lavender	821	Lesser	795	Spurrey, Corn	171
Milkwort	657	Sloe	297	Knotted	148
Pink	824, 825	Smallreed, Narrow	1188	Sandwort	170
Purslane	153	Purple	1187	Squill, Autumn	1043
Rocket	110	Wood	1186	Bluebell	1044
Sedge, Sweet	943	Smyrnium, Common	453	Spring	1042
Sedum, Biting	366	Snake root	872	Squinancywort	480
English	362	Snakes-head	1035	Squirrel-tail Grass	1208
Hairy	365	Snakeweed	872	Stachys, Betony	798
Orpine	361	Snapdragon, Great	730	Downy	799
Rock	368	Lesser	730	Field	802
Roseroot	360	Sneezewort	530	Hedge	800
Tasteless	367	Snowdrop	1024	Marsh	801
Thick-leaved	363	Snowflake	1025	Star-fruit	972
White	364	Soapwort	132	Star of Bethlehem	1039
Selaginella, Common	1260	Solanum, Bittersweet	713	Yellow	1038
Self-heal	793	Black	714	Star thistle	574
Senebiera, Common	107	Solomon-seal, Angular	1030	Starwort, Bog	166
Lesser	108	Common	1029	Chickweed	165
Senecio, Broad-leaved	548	Whorled	1028	Great	169
Fen	547	Sorrel	864	Lesser	167
Field	550	Mountain	866	Marsh	168
Groundsel	540	Sheep's	865	Water	163
Marsh	549	Wood	216	Wood	164
Narrow-leaved	546	Sowbread	651	Statice, Common	821
Ragwort	545	Sowthistle, Common	592	Matted	823
Squalid	543	Corn	590	Rock	822
Viscous	541	Marsh	591	St. Dabeoc's Heath	633
Water	544	Sparganium, Branched	939	St. John's-wort	180
Wood	542	Simple	940	St. Patrick's Cabbage	385
Service-tree, Wild	336	Small	941	Stinking May-weed	526
Seseli, Mountain	427	Spartina, Card	1201	Stitchwort	169
Sesleria, Blue	1253	Spearwort	12	Lesser	167
Setter-wort	27	Great	11	Stock, Common	48
Sheep's-bit	612	Spear-thistle	560	Queen	48
Sheep-sorrel	865	Speedwell	748—763	Sea	49
Shepherd's-needle	439	Spleenwort, Alternate	1298	Stonecrop	360
Purse	101	Black	1296	Biting	366
Sherardia, Blue	481	Common	1294	Stork's-bill	213—215
Shieldfern, Broad	1288	Forked	1299	Strapwort	832
Crested	1287	Green	1295	Stratiotes, Water	978

INDEX.

	FIG.
Strawberry, Wild	311
-tree	628
Suæda, Herbaceous	839
Shrubby	838
Succory	607
Lamb's	608
Swine's	608
Sulphur-weed	433
Sundew, Common	390
English	392
Oblong	391
Sweet-briar	330
Flag	943
Gale	908
Sedge	943
Swine-cress	107
Swine's Succory	608
Sycamore	221
Tamarisc, Common	175
Tamus	1026
Tansy	533
Tare	277
Teasel, Fuller's	490
Small	491
Wild	490
Teesdalia, Common	98
Thalecress	60
Thalictrum, Alpine	2
Lesser	3
Yellow	4
Thesium, Flax-leaved	881
Thistle, Carline	569
Cotton	568
Creeping	562
Dwarf	567
Marsh	561
Meadow	566
Melancholy	564
Milk	556
Musk	557
Scotch	568
Slender	559
Spear	560
Star	574
Tuberous	565
Welted	558
Woolly	563
Thornapple	711
Thrift, Common	824
Plantain	825
Thyme, Basil	788
Water	976
Wild	786
Tillæa, Mossy	358
Timothy-grass	1167
Toadflax	732
Bastard	881
Ivy-leaved	737
Tofieldia, Marsh	1056
Toothwort	723
Touch-me-not	218
Tower Mustard	56
Towercress	57
Traveller's Joy	1
Treacle Mustard	73
Tree Mallow	194
Trefoil, Bird's-foot	265

	FIG.
Trefoil, Buckbean	681
Hare's-foot	246
Hop	262
Marsh	681
Triadia, Decumbent	1251
Trichomanes, European	1308
Trientale, Common	656
Triglochio, Marsh	974
Sea	975
Trigonel, Bird's-foot	243
Trinia, Common	406
Trollius, Globe	25
Tulip, Wild	1036
Turnip	79
Swedish	79
Tutsan	129
Twayblade	987
Lesser	988
Vaccinium, Bilberry	624
Bog	625
Cowberry	626
Cranberry	627
Valerian, Cat's	484
Greek	683
Marsh	483
Pyrenean	485
Red	482
Spur	482
Venus's-comb	439
Veronica, Alpine	750
Brooklime	754
Buxbaum's	760
Common	752
Fingered	763
Germander	757
Ivy	758
Marsh	755
Mountain	756
Procumbent	759
Rock	749
Spiked	748
Thyme-leaved	751
Vernal	762
Wall	761
Water	753
Vervain	820
Vetch, Bithynian	286
Bitter	281
Bush	282
Common	284
Grass	287
Hairy	277
Horse-shoe	275
Kidney	267
Milk	270
Slender	278
Spring	285
Tufted	279
Upright	281
Wood	280
Yellow	283
Vetchling	287
Yellow	288
Vileurnum, Mealy	452
Guelder Rose	463
Violet, Dame's	68

	FIG.
Violet, Dog	124
Hairy	122
Marsh	120
Pansy	125
Sand	123
Sweet	121
Water	647
Viper's Bugloss	690
Wake Robin	942
Wallcress	60
Wallflower	50
Wall-Pepper	366
Wallrue	1297
Wartcress	107
Watercress, Common	52
Creeping	53
Great	55
Marsh	54
Water Dropwort	421
Hemlock	401
Lily, White	34
Yellow	35
Milfoil	393
Parsnip	413
Pepper	176
Plantain	969
Purslane	356
Soldier	978
Starwort	900
Thyme	976
Violet	647
Wort	176, 177
Waybent	1207
Wayfaring-tree	462
Weather-glass, Poor Man's	658
Shepherd's	658
Weld	113
Welsh Poppy	41
Whin	226
Petty	230
White Beam-tree	335
Bottle	134
White-rot	396
Whitethorn	338
Whitlow-grass	92
Whortleberry	624
Red	626
Willow, Almond	919
Bay	916
Bedford	917
Common	918
Crack	917
Creeping	925
Downy	926
Dwarf	930
French	341, 919
Goat	922
Golden	918
Herb	341—349
Osier	921
Purple	920
Reticulate	929
Rose	920
Round-eared	923
Sallow	922
Tea-leaved	924

346   INDEX.

	FIG.		FIG.		FIG.
Willow, White . W.	918	Woodsia, Alpine	1307	Yellow Archangel	812
Whortle . . .	928	Woodruff . .	479	Centaury . .	680
Woolly . . .	927	Woodrush, Curved	1077	Cress . . .	55
Wintercress, American	51	Field . .	1078	Rattle . .	76S
Common . . .	51	Great . .	1076	Rocket . .	51
Wintergreen, Common	644	Hairy . .	1075	Weed . .	113
Intermediate . .	643	Spiked . .	1079	Wort . .	680
Larger . . .	642	Wood-sage . .	813	Yew . . .	936
One-flowered . .	641	Wood-sorrel .	216		
Serrated . . .	645	Wormwood .	537		
Woad, Dyer's . .	109	Woundwort .	799	Zannichellia .	954
Wolfsbane . . .	30			Zostera, Common	949
Wood Betony . .	798			Dwarf . .	950
Woodbine . . .	464	Yarrow . .	531		

www.ingramcontent.com/pod-product-compliance
Lightning Source LLC
Chambersburg PA
CBHW031432230426
43668CB00007B/504